D1300212

Babe & Kris Winkelman's

Great
Fish & Game
Recipes

Fish, Venison, Gamebird and Side Dish Recipes
From Easy to Elegant

CREATIVE
PUBLISHING
international

CHANHASSEN, MINNESOTA

www.creativepub.com

BABE WINKELMAN is nationally known as a successful
sportsman and through his television shows, *Good Fishing*™
and *Outdoor Secrets*™, and his hunting and fishing columns.
KRIS WINKELMAN hosts the popular television cooking
segment, "Kris' Kitchen."

They live in northern Minnesota.

FOREWORD FROM KRIS

I GREW UP BELIEVING YOU DON'T KILL ANYTHING YOU
DON'T PLAN TO EAT. THAT'S WHY I'VE WORKED SO
HARD TO DEVELOP RECIPES THE ENTIRE FAMILY CAN ENJOY.
THE JOB STARTS WITH PROPER CARE AND HANDLING OF
THE MEAT FROM THE FIELD OR LAKE TO THE FREEZER.
WHEN SPORTSMEN COMPLAIN THAT THEIR WALLEYE
TASTES "FISHY" OR THEIR VENISON "SMELLS FUNNY,"
I USUALLY SUSPECT IT'S BECAUSE THEY DIDN'T GIVE
ADEQUATE ATTENTION TO THE CLEANING, TRANSPORTING,
PACKAGING AND FREEZING OF THE GAME.

PREPARING THE GAME IS THE NEXT STEP. WILD GAME
IS, BY NATURE, LEANER THAN DOMESTIC MEAT, AND
THAT MEANS IT MUST BE PREPARED DIFFERENTLY. THE
RECIPES IN THIS COOKBOOK ARE DESIGNED TO YIELD
MOIST, FLAVORFUL DISHES WITHOUT SACRIFICING THE
DISTINCTIVE FLAVOR OF THE GAME.

IT'S MY SINCERE HOPE THAT YOUR FAMILY WILL ENJOY
THE RECIPES IN THIS COOKBOOK AS MUCH AS BABE,
KARLEE AND I HAVE ENJOYED THEM.

Copyright © 2004 by Creative Publishing international, Inc.
18705 Lake Drive East
Chanhassen, MN 55317
1-800-328-3895
www.creativepub.com

All rights reserved.

President/CEO: Michael Eleftheriou
Vice President/Publisher: Linda Ball
Vice President/Retail Sales & Marketing: Kevin Haas
Executive Editor, Outdoor Group: Barbara Harold
Creative Director: Brad Springer
Recipe Editor: Teresa Marrone
Project Manager: Tracy Stanley
Studio Services Manager: Jeanette Moss McCurdy
Photographer: Tate Carlson
Assistant Photographer: Herb Schnabel
Prop Stylist: Bobbette Parker
Food Stylist: Sue Brue
Asssistant Food Stylist: Pegi Lee
Director, Production Services: Kim Gerber
Production Manager: Laura Hokkanen
Production Staff: Helga Thielen

Printed on American paper by: R. R. Donnelley
10 9 8 7 6 5 4 3 2 1

BABE & KRIS WINKELMAN'S
GREAT GAME & FISH RECIPES
by Babe & Kris Winkelman

Contributing Photographers: Dan Nelson, Michael Aulie,
Sothers Photography

Library of Congress Cataloging-in-Publication Data

Winkelman, Babe.
    Babe & Kris Winkelman's great fish & game recipes / by
Babe Winkelman and Kris Winkelman.
        p. cm.
    Includes index.
    ISBN 1-58923-136-8
    1. Cookery (Fish) 2. Cookery (Game) I. Winkelman,
Kris. II. Title.

TX747.W5596 2003
641.6'91--dc22

2003055441

BABE & KRIS WINKELMAN'S
GREAT FISH & GAME RECIPES

CONTENTS

A Note from Kris' Kitchen

A wise man said that happiness isn't a destination, it's a journey. This cookbook is dedicated to the millions of hunters and anglers who understand that tagging a deer or catching a limit of fish isn't the end of the journey, it's only the beginning.

This book was written for those outdoor aficionados who have discovered that transforming a bag of frozen venison into a gourmet meal can be every bit as challenging and rewarding as bagging the deer; and for those who experiment with recipes as enthusiastically as they seek out new fishing holes.

It is not the goal of this cookbook to turn sportsmen into French chefs, nor is it our intention to pass along "Grandma's favorite game recipes." Modern chefs prepare pen-raised, fattened game more akin to aged beef than wild venison, and Grandma's venison and duck were so dry and chewy they were barely edible. The game in our freezers requires a different approach, and in preparing this book we've searched for techniques that bring out the best in the wild harvest.

The decision to write this book was easy. Ever since I started the "Kris' Kitchen" feature on Babe's *Good Fishing*™ and *Outdoor Secrets*™ television shows, I've literally been overwhelmed with letters, e-mails and phone calls from viewers requesting a game and fish cookbook. Eating wild game, it seems, has become an obsession with the country's 50

million anglers and 16 million hunters.

I'm guessing this growing passion for outdoor cuisine has a lot to do with demographics. The average sportsman is around 50 years of age and has been enjoying the outdoors for 40 years. As the sporting public matures, individuals tend to be less concerned about trophies and limits and more focused on the total experience. For many of us, preparing and eating the fish and game we collect has become a big part of that experience.

The growing popularity of game in restaurants has been another factor. Dishes like venison medallions, roast Long Island duckling, braised pheasant and baked walleye are showing up on the menus of fine dining establishments everywhere. Eating gourmet dishes prepared by qualified chefs taught us that venison doesn't have to taste like liver and duck needn't be as dry and flavorless as a loaf of week-old bread.

Admittedly, the venison and duck served in restaurants isn't the same as the game we bring home from our weekend outings. It's pen-raised, fattened and, in the case of Long Island duckling, not even the same species. On the other hand, if the chefs at those restaurants overcooked game the way many sportsmen do, the final product would be as dry, tough and disagreeable as the venison fixed in kitchens across the country every day.

The goal of many home cooks is to make venison taste like beef

and pheasant taste like chicken. That's a mistake, because wild game has a rich, distinct flavor all its own—a flavor meant to be accentuated, not masked. Those who have uncovered the secrets to preparing wild game often find they enjoy venison more than beef and prefer pheasant, quail and ruffed grouse to chicken.

In writing this cookbook, I've attempted to find a happy middle ground between the complicated recipes used by professional chefs utilizing hard-to-find ingredients, and the smother-it-in-cream-of-mushroom-soup recipes most of us grew up with. Many of the meals require a bit more preparation time. After all, no one expects to take a deer in 15 minutes, so why would anyone think they could put together a delicious meal that quickly? But we've also included a number of quick and easy recipes for cooks on the go.

Some of the recipes in this cookbook were provided by friends and acquaintances across the continent. We started picking up recipes at the lodges we visited in the making of our television shows. Hunting and fishing companions offered their favorite dishes, as did dinner guests at our home.

We watched television cooking shows, studied cookbooks and scoured the Internet for recipe ideas. Most of the recipes we found—fully three-fourths of them—simply didn't work on wild game. Of the rest, nearly all had to be tweaked in one way or another.

Along the way we discovered that getting there is, indeed, half the fun. The countless days we've spent in the kitchen developing recipes have been every bit as enjoyable as the days devoted to harvesting that game.

Every serious hunter or angler knows what it's like to watch a glorious sunset at the end of a special day in the field or on the water. Fortunately, those memorable outings don't have to end at sunset. After the rods and guns have been put away, grilling a venison steak or frying up a batch of crappies is the perfect way to relive those wonderful days afield.

That lesson certainly hasn't been lost on Bob Musil, executive director of the Red Wing (Minnesota) Convention and Visitor's Bureau. Bob sent along a recipe for baked pheasant with asparagus and bleu cheese which began, "Uncork a bottle of white wine and pour yourself a glass, taking care to reserve at least 1/4 cup for the recipe." After putting the dish in the oven, he suggests, "Pour yourself another glass of wine; you deserve it." Finally, he says to cook the dish "approximately 50 minutes or until sauce is bubbly and wine is gone."

And that, folks, is the right approach to preparing game and fish. Take your time, do it right, savor the moment and most of all, enjoy!

Kris Winkelman

Those who know me may wonder why I'm listed as co-author of this cookbook. After all, everyone knows it's Kris—not me—who does most of the cooking in our house.

On the other hand, I believe that preparing game and fish should be a family activity. Sharing in the preparation and enjoyment of nature's bounty is a very important part of the outdoor experience, and I hope that lending my name to the book will encourage other sportsmen to get involved in the process.

Some people think it's women—not men—who do all the cooking. I don't believe that. I know a lot of men who enjoy preparing fish and game, just as I know a lot of women who enjoy hunting and fishing.

Kris is one of those women. She's been with me on dozens of hunting and fishing trips. She has taken trophy mule deer, bagged limits of pheasants and partridge and caught some monster fish.

When it comes to the outdoors, there is no division of chores. Gone are the days when men bring home the meat and women fix it. Women are joining the ranks of hunters and anglers in record numbers, and I think that's great. An increasing number of men can be found grilling venison steaks or frying up a batch of fish fillets, and I think that's great, too. I'm convinced that outdoor cuisine and outdoor adventure are best shared with family, and I'm glad Kris feels the same.

I encourage men and women to take at least one night a week to experiment with a new fish or game recipe. Make a night of it. Pop the cork on a bottle of wine, try one of the recipes from this book and relive your adventures in the great outdoors with family and friends.

It's a wonderful way to spend an evening.

BABE WINKELMAN

CHAPTER ONE

TAKING STOCK
The Foundation
of the Kitchen

WHAT DO PROFESSIONAL CHEFS KNOW THAT THE REST OF US DON'T? WHY IS THE VENISON, DUCK AND PHEASANT SERVED IN FINE RESTAURANTS SO MOIST, TENDER AND FLAVORFUL?

For one thing, the game prepared in professional kitchens is raised commercially; the controlled diet provided on the game farm ensures that the meat has more fat (which makes the meat juicier) and a milder flavor than that from its wild cousins. But that's only part of the answer. Any good chef could take game from your freezer and turn it into a meal fit for a king. So what's their secret?

Aside from the fact that they're trained chefs, the "secret" ingredient found in most professional kitchens is the stock used in preparing soups, braising, poaching and stewing meat. These homemade stocks also are the foundation for the delicious sauces that accompany most meals.

Let's discuss exactly what we mean when we refer to "stock." The French term for stock is *fonds de cuisine,* which translates into "the foundation of the kitchen." Stock is made by simmering the bones and meat of fish, birds or animals along with vegetables and seasonings (a common seasoning is a bundle of herbs called a *bouquet garni*). I've interviewed many chefs over the years, and every one has affirmed that a well-tended stock is the heart and soul of wild game cookery.

If there's one thing I learned in preparing this cookbook it's that braising, stewing or poaching meat in the appropriate stock produces the moistest, most flavorful dishes imaginable, and those same stocks can be used to make wonderful sauces and gravies that further accentuate the flavor of the dish. I use stock rather than water to boil wild rice, steam vegetables and moisten stuffing, all with exceptional results.

If stocks are the "secret ingredient" in wild game cookery, they must be difficult to make, right? Actually, stocks are very simple to prepare, requiring little more than peeling a few vegetables and occasionally skimming the froth from the surface early in the simmering process. The finished stock can be frozen for months, and thawed whenever you plan to make a special dish.

Doesn't canned chicken broth or beef broth produce the same results? While store-bought broth will work, it doesn't have the flavor or richness of home-made stock. Besides, using canned chicken broth will lend a chicken flavor to your pheasant, grouse or quail. In a pinch, however, it's possible to "enhance" a canned broth by simmering it with your preferred herbs and spices, and perhaps some fresh vegetables.

Preparing stocks is also a great way to utilize those parts of the game that might normally go to waste. Leg, shank or shoulder bones of a deer that would normally be discarded are perfect for making stock. Upland bird hunters who typically breast their game can use the carcass to prepare a delicious stock. Sportsmen who've been looking for a way to utilize the legs of gamebirds need look no further. These "spare parts" can be frozen until the day you decide to make stock.

If you really want to stretch your food budget, you can pick the meat from the bones after simmering for stock and use it in another recipe (you may want to do this relatively early on in the stock-making process, while the meat still has some flavor; then, return the bones to the stockpot and continue simmering). For example, you can salvage enough meat from two pheasant carcasses to fix such delicious dishes as Pheasant Dinner Pie (page 93) or pheasant and dumplings.

When visiting the meat department at the grocery store, watch for sales on chicken legs and inexpensive cuts of meat or soup bones. Put them in the freezer, and add them to the pot next time you simmer up a fresh batch of stock. If you serve chicken or turkey, save the carcass in a zipper-style plastic bag in the freezer until you're ready to make stock.

Preparing a good stock usually

takes only a few hours, and during most of that time it just sits there and simmers. Once you've cut up the vegetables and skimmed a bit of froth, it's a hands-off operation.

Many of the recipes in this cookbook call for venison stock or gamebird stock. If you don't have them, you can substitute beef broth or chicken broth, but I suspect you'd be far more satisfied with the results if you used homemade stock.

TIPS FOR PREPARING STOCK

• Always use cold water and heat it very slowly.

• Never allow the water to boil.

• Use only enough water to cover the bones. As the water cooks away, add more as needed to keep the bones covered.

• During the first hour or so, carefully skim the froth from the surface.

• Don't touch or stir the ingredients during simmering.

• Never cover the stockpot.

• When straining at the end, don't press the vegetables. Rather, allow them to drain naturally.

• Allow the strained stock to cool, preferably in a sink of ice, then refrigerate. Stock is a perfect medium for bacteria, so don't allow it to sit around at room temperature for long.

• Store stock for 3 to 4 days, covered, in the refrigerator. If you need to store it longer than that, bring it to a simmer, skim and return to the refrigerator for another 3 to 4 days, or freeze in convenient portions.

BROWN GAMEBIRD STOCK

Carcasses of 2 or 3 upland gamebirds or waterfowl

1 medium onion, coarsely chopped

2 carrots, coarsely chopped

1 rib celery, coarsely chopped

BOUQUET GARNI:

2 bay leaves

A few sprigs of fresh parsley

10 whole peppercorns

1 tablespoon (1 g) dried parsley flakes

A sprig or 2 of fresh thyme, or 1 teaspoon (.8 g) dried

1 large clove garlic, crushed

Heat oven to 400°F (205°C). Thoroughly wash carcasses; separate wings, breast, back and thighs. Carefully cut away any excess fat. Place gamebird pieces in large roasting pan. Roast, uncovered, for 45 minutes to 1 hour, or until completely browned; turn occasionally with tongs to ensure even browning.

Once the pieces are browned, add onion, carrots and celery to roaster. Continue roasting until vegetables are browned, stirring frequently. Meanwhile, place all bouquet garni ingredients on square of cheesecloth; wrap and tie with kitchen twine and set aside.

When vegetables have browned, transfer gamebird pieces and vegetables to large stockpot. Place roaster on a burner over high heat and add 1 quart (.95 l) of water. Deglaze by scraping caramelized bits off bottom of roaster with wooden spoon. Pour mixture into stockpot (it will look like dark-colored water). Add enough additional water to cover bird parts and heat to simmering—do not boil. Adjust heat to maintain simmer and cook for 45 minutes, skimming froth with spoon and ladling off any fat that floats to surface. After about 45 minutes, add bouquet garni. Continue cooking, uncovered, for 3 hours longer, adding water as necessary to keep bones covered. Strain stock through wire-mesh strainer lined with cheesecloth and cool at room temperature. Refrigerate overnight.

The next day, scrape off and discard any fat that has congealed on surface. Freeze stock in convenient portions,* or refrigerate for 3 or 4 days before using (if refrigerating for longer period, reheat stock after 4 days, skim, and return to refrigerator).

*FREEZING TIP
I like to freeze stock in 2- and 3-cup (4.6 and 6.9 dl) plastic food-storage containers. Be sure to mark the lid with the type of stock.

TAKING STOCK
8

WHITE GAMEBIRD STOCK

Carcasses of 2 or 3 upland gamebirds or waterfowl

1 medium onion, coarsely chopped

2 carrots, coarsely chopped

1 rib celery, coarsely chopped

Bouquet garni (see Brown Gamebird Stock, page 8)

Thoroughly wash carcasses; separate wings, breast, back and thighs. Carefully cut away any excess fat. Place gamebird pieces, onion, carrots and celery in large stockpot; add enough cold water to cover gamebird pieces and vegetables. Heat to simmering—do not boil. Adjust heat to maintain simmer and cook for 45 minutes, skimming froth with spoon and ladling off any fat that floats to surface.

After stock has simmered for about 45 minutes, add bouquet garni. Continue cooking, uncovered, for 3 hours longer, adding water as necessary to keep bones covered. Strain, refrigerate and freeze as described in Brown Gamebird Stock, page 8.

VENISON STOCK

3 to 4 pounds (1.36 to 1.8 kg) venison bones, preferably with some meat

1 medium onion, coarsely chopped

2 carrots, coarsely chopped

2 ribs celery, coarsely chopped

Bouquet garni (see Brown Gamebird Stock, page 8)

Heat oven to 400°F (205°C). Place bones in large roasting pan. Roast, uncovered, for 45 minutes to 1 hour, or until browned; turn occasionally with tongs to ensure even browning.

Once the bones are browned, add onion, carrots and celery to roaster. Continue roasting until vegetables are browned, stirring frequently. When vegetables have browned, transfer bones and vegetables to large stockpot. Place roaster on a burner over high heat and add 2 cups (4.6 dl) water. Deglaze by scraping caramelized bits off bottom of roaster with wooden spoon. Pour mixture into stockpot (it will look like dark-colored water). Add enough additional water to generously cover bones and heat to simmering—do not boil. Adjust heat to maintain simmer and cook for 1 hour, skimming froth with spoon and ladling off any fat that floats to surface. After about 1 hour, add bouquet garni. Continue cooking, uncovered, for 5 hours longer, adding water as necessary to keep bones covered.

Strain, refrigerate and freeze as described in Brown Gamebird Stock, page 8.

GAMEBIRD STOCK IN A PRESSURE COOKER

Cooks who don't have time to tend a stock for several hours might want to consider using a pressure cooker. It takes a lot less time and still produces a great stock.

Carcasses of 2 or 3 upland gamebirds or waterfowl

1 tablespoon (15 ml) vegetable oil

1 medium onion, coarsely chopped

1 carrot, coarsely chopped

1 rib celery, coarsely chopped

1/2 teaspoon (.4 g) dried thyme

6 whole peppercorns

A few sprigs of fresh parsley

2 bay leaves

1 large clove garlic, chopped

Thoroughly wash carcasses. Separate wings, breast, back and thighs; pat dry. Carefully cut away any excess fat. In pressure cooker, brown gamebird pieces in oil over medium heat.

Transfer gamebird pieces to plate; pour off excess fat from cooker if necessary. Add onion, carrot and celery to cooker; sauté until browned. Add 2 cups (4.6 dl) water and cook for a few minutes, stirring to loosen browned bits. Return gamebird pieces to cooker; add thyme, peppercorns, parsley, bay leaves and garlic. Add 2 quarts (1.9 l) water. Lock lid in place and set pressure for 15 pounds. Heat over high heat until control jiggles; once pressure is up, adjust heat to maintain pressure (see manufacturer's recommendations) and cook for 20 minutes. Reduce heat and pressure in cooker as directed by manufacturer until cool enough to remove lid. Release pressure and remove lid. Return uncovered cooker to heat and simmer for 1 hour longer.

Strain, refrigerate and freeze as described in Brown Gamebird Stock, page 8.

VENISON STOCK IN A PRESSURE COOKER

3 to 4 pounds (1.36 to 1.8 kg) venison bones, preferably with some meat

1 tablespoon (15 ml) vegetable oil

1 medium onion, coarsely chopped

1 carrot, coarsely chopped

1 rib celery, coarsely chopped

1 large clove garlic, coarsely chopped

1/2 teaspoon (.4 g) dried thyme

10 whole peppercorns

A few springs of fresh parsley

2 bay leaves

In pressure cooker, brown venison bones in oil over medium heat. Transfer bones to plate; pour off excess fat if necessary.

Add onion, carrot, celery and garlic to cooker; sauté until browned. Add 2 cups (4.6 dl) water and cook for a few minutes, stirring to loosen browned bits. Return bones to cooker; add thyme, peppercorns, parsley and bay leaves. Add 2 quarts (1.9 l) water. Lock lid in place and set pressure for 15 pounds. Heat over high heat until control jiggles; once pressure is up, adjust heat to maintain pressure (see manufacturer's recommendations) and cook for 20 minutes. Reduce heat and pressure in cooker as directed by manufacturer until cool enough to remove lid. Release pressure and remove lid. Return uncovered cooker to heat and simmer for 1 hour longer.

Strain, refrigerate and freeze as described in Brown Gamebird Stock, page 8.

FISH STOCK

Making a fish stock is easier than you might think. A good homemade stock not only is an important ingredient in a number of delicious sauces, it also makes a wonderful poaching liquid.

2 pounds (900 g) fish frames*

1 onion, thinly sliced

1 cup (2.3 dl) dry white wine

1 teaspoon (15 ml) lemon juice

6 fresh parsley stems (not the leaves), optional

Salt to taste

In large stockpot, combine all ingredients. Add cold water to cover fish frames. Heat to simmering over medium heat; adjust heat and simmer, uncovered, for 30 minutes. Strain stock through wire-mesh strainer lined with cheesecloth and cool at room temperature. Refrigerate overnight; the next day, strain stock again. Freeze as described in Brown Gamebird Stock, page 8.

> ## *FISH FRAMES
> *Be sure to remove the gills, skin, fins, tail and stomach lining from the fish. You want just the heads, bones and whatever meat was left after cleaning.*

EMERGENCY FISH STOCK

If a recipe calls for a fish stock and you have none, you can always make an "emergency" stock. This quick-and-easy stock tastes almost as good as the real thing. Bottled clam juice—the key ingredient—is available at most grocery stores.

1¹/₂ cups (3.5 dl) bottled clam juice

1 cup (2.3 dl) water

1 cup (2.3 dl) dry white wine

1 onion, thinly sliced

6 fresh parsley stems (not the leaves), optional

Combine all ingredients in saucepan. Heat to simmering over medium heat; adjust heat and simmer, uncovered, for 30 minutes. Strain stock through wire-mesh strainer lined with cheesecloth and cool at room temperature. Use within 2 days.

FISH
RECIPES

CHAPTER TWO

WHILE THIS BOOK IS PRIMARILY FOR PEOPLE WHO CATCH THEIR OWN FISH, IT'S ALSO GREAT FOR THE COOK WHO BUYS FISH AT THE STORE.

Many gamefish, including walleye, trout, catfish, perch and northern pike, are sold over the counter at supermarkets and fish markets across the country. And the list of available fish is increasing daily as frequent air shipping brings exotic species closer to home.

As long as it's fresh or was properly frozen, fish is easily turned into a delicious meal. Most of us have our favorite recipes and they almost always turn out great.

If one of the recipes in this book calls for a species of fish you don't have, the substitution chart in the Appendix (page 119) lists alternates.

TIPS FOR PREPARING FISH

• If the fish is fresh, rinse each piece under a sprayer until it's thoroughly washed and free of any slime.

• If the fish is frozen, remove it from the container or bag, wash thoroughly and store in the refrigerator, preferably on ice.

• Never allow fresh or frozen fish to sit in water.

• The temperature of cooking oil for frying fish should be around 350°F (175°C). Shake the pan frequently to make sure the fillets have an adequate amount of oil under them.

• The most basic coating for frying fish is seasoned flour. Breadcrumbs, beer batter or a commercial breading can also be used.

Cajun Catfish Tortellini

This recipe isn't just for catfish; it works well with walleye and a host of other freshwater fish as well. It's important to use the best tortellini you can find, and to use finely grated fresh Parmesan cheese. Pre-grated Parmesan doesn't incorporate into the sauce as well as fresh-grated.

1 cup (140 g) all-purpose flour

2 tablespoons (12 g) Cajun seasoning blend (see below), plus additional for seasoning fish

2 boneless, skinless catfish fillets (1¹/₂ to 2 pounds/ 680 to 900 g each)

³/₄ cup (165 g/1¹/₂ sticks) butter, divided

2 packages (9 ounces/255 g each) refrigerated cheese tortellini

2 cups (180 g) broccoli florets

1 cup (2.3 dl) heavy cream

1 cup (125 g) freshly grated Parmesan cheese

3 tablespoons (27 g) pine nuts, optional

Heat oven to 190°F (88°C). In mixing bowl, combine flour and 2 tablespoons (12 g) Cajun seasoning; stir to blend. Rinse fillets; pat dry with paper towels. Sprinkle fillets with additional Cajun seasoning to taste; dredge in seasoned flour. In large skillet, melt ¹/₄ cup (55 g/half of a stick) butter over medium heat. When butter stops foaming, add floured fillets. Cook until golden brown on both sides. Transfer fillets to plate; place in oven while you prepare pasta, broccoli and sauce.

Cook tortellini according to package directions; drain and set aside. In saucepan, heat about 1 cup (2.3 dl) water over high heat until boiling. Place colander or sieve over saucepan. Add broccoli; cover and steam until just beginning to soften. Remove colander from saucepan and set aside.

In skillet used to fry fish, melt remaining ¹/₂ cup (110 g/1 stick) butter over medium-high heat. Add cream and heat to boiling. Reduce heat to medium; add drained tortellini, broccoli, Parmesan cheese and pine nuts, stirring gently to combine. To serve, place pasta mixture in center of individual plates; surround with a few pieces of fried fish.

Cajun Seasoning Blend

You may use a commercial seasoning blend, or make your own by combining:

1 tablespoon (7.5 g) garlic powder

1 tablespoon (6 g) freshly ground black pepper

1 tablespoon (7.5 g) onion powder

2 teaspoons (1.5 g) dried thyme

1 teaspoon (2 g) cayenne pepper

¹/₂ teaspoon (.2 g) dried oregano

NORTHERN PIKE WITH MUSTARD-DILL SAUCE

Pity the poor northern pike. It just doesn't get any respect. For whatever reason, anglers across the pike's range determined it was not fit for the table. Perhaps it's those Y-bones that many anglers don't know how to remove, or those razor-sharp teeth. Or maybe the pike's particular odor or its slimy skin prompted anglers to treat pike as second-class citizens. Whatever the case, pike is actually one of the tastiest of all gamefish, as anyone who tries this recipe will agree. The sauce may seem a little strong, but it is the perfect accompaniment.

4 to 6 boneless, skinless northern pike fillets or fillet portions* (about 6 ounces/ 170 g each)

A squirt of lemon juice

Salt and pepper

2 eggs

1 cup (125 g) freshly grated Parmesan cheese

All-purpose flour, approximately 1 cup (140 g)

Fresh breadcrumbs (page 118), approximately 1½ cups (65 g)

Clarified butter (page 118) for frying

MUSTARD-DILL SAUCE:

2 cups (4.6 dl) chicken broth

3 tablespoons (45 g) butter, divided

2 tablespoons (15 g) flour

¼ cup (60 ml) heavy cream

1 tablespoon (15 g) Dijon mustard, or to taste

Snipped fresh dill weed, or dried dill weed

A squirt of lemon juice

Salt and pepper

Heat oven to 190°F (88°C). Rinse fillets; pat dry with paper towels. Season with lemon juice, salt and pepper to taste. In large mixing bowl, beat eggs with fork; add Parmesan cheese and beat until well mixed. Place flour in flat dish; place breadcrumbs in another flat dish. Dredge fillets in flour, shaking off excess. Dip into egg mixture, allowing excess to drip off. Coat with breadcrumbs. In large nonstick skillet, melt butter over medium-high heat. Add breaded fillets and cook until golden brown on each side. Transfer fillets to plate; place in oven while you prepare sauce.

To prepare the sauce: In small saucepan, heat broth to boiling over medium-high heat. While broth is heating, melt 2 tablespoons (30 g) butter in another small saucepan over low heat. Stirring constantly, sprinkle flour into butter; cook, stirring constantly, until mixture thickens. When broth boils, add flour-butter mixture slowly to broth, stirring constantly. When thoroughly incorporated, add cream gradually. Stir in mustard and dill to taste; sauce should be strongly flavored. Finish sauce by adding remaining 1 tablespoon (15 g) butter, lemon juice, and salt and pepper to taste. Serve sauce with fish.

> ***PIKE FILLET PREPARATION**
> *Remove the rib bones, Y-bones and lateral line from the pike. If the fillets are very long, cut into shorter portions so they'll be easy to handle.*

PARMESAN FISH WITH ALFREDO SAUCE

4 TO 6 SERVINGS

This is an elegant dish that's sure to please the pasta lovers in any family. It works equally well with walleye, crappie, perch, bass or just about any gamefish. Serve with garlic toast and a good Chardonnay or Riesling wine.

1 cup (40 g) fresh breadcrumbs (page 118)

1½ cups (188 g) freshly grated Parmesan cheese, divided

1 tablespoon (4 g) chopped fresh parsley, optional

2 large eggs

2 tablespoons (30 ml) milk

1½ to 2 pounds (680 to 900 g) boneless, skinless fish fillets

½ cup (110 g) clarified butter (page 118)

2 packages (9 ounces/255 g each) refrigerated cheese tortellini, or 1 pound (454 g) plain fettuccini

2 cups (180 g) broccoli florets

½ cup (110 g/1 stick) butter

1 cup (2.3 dl) heavy cream

Salt and pepper

3 tablespoons (27 g) pine nuts

In mixing bowl, combine breadcrumbs, ½ cup (63 g) Parmesan cheese and the parsley; stir to mix well. In another bowl, beat eggs and milk together. Rinse fillets; pat dry with paper towels. Dip fillets into egg mixture, allowing excess to drip off. Coat with breadcrumbs, firmly packing crumbs onto fillets with your fingertips. Arrange on plate; cover with plastic wrap and refrigerate for 1 hour or longer.

When you're ready to cook, heat oven to 190°F (88°C). In large non-stick skillet, melt clarified butter over medium heat. Add breaded fillets; cook until golden brown on both sides. Transfer fillets to clean plate; place in oven while you prepare pasta, broccoli and sauce.

Cook tortellini according to package directions; drain and set aside. In saucepan, heat about 1 cup (2.3 dl) water over high heat until boiling. Place colander or sieve over saucepan. Add broccoli; cover and steam until just beginning to soften. Remove colander from saucepan and set aside.

In large skillet, melt butter over medium heat. Add cream, the remaining Parmesan cheese, and salt and pepper to taste; stir to blend. Add drained pasta, broccoli and the pine nuts to sauce. To serve, place pasta mixture in center of individual plates; surround with a few pieces of fried fish.

FISH TACOS

Specific amounts aren't given for this recipe because it's so simple. Just fry up the amount of fish you need for the number of people you'll be serving, and top the tacos the way you like.

Boneless, skinless fish fillets (or skin-on, scaled fillets)

Seasoning salt, plain salt and pepper

Eggs (1 egg will coat ½ to ¾ pound/225 to 340 g fillets; use as many as you need)

Milk (1 tablespoon/15 ml per egg)

Crushed cracker crumbs (½ cup/35 g will coat ½ to ¾ pound/225 to 340 g fillets)

Vegetable oil for frying

Hard-shell (corn) taco shells

Shredded cheddar and/or Monterey Jack cheese

Salsa

Shredded or chopped lettuce

Sour cream

Heat oven to 325°F (163°C). Rinse fillets; pat dry with paper towels. Sprinkle fillets with seasoning salt, plain salt and pepper to taste. In bowl, beat together egg(s) with 1 tablespoon (15 ml) milk or water per egg. Dip fish fillets into egg mixture, allowing excess to drip off. Coat with cracker crumbs. Coat bottom of large nonstick skillet generously with oil; heat over medium-high heat until oil shimmers. Add fillets; cook until golden on both sides.

Stuff taco shells with fried fish; top with cheese and salsa. Place on baking sheet and bake until cheese melts. Top with lettuce and sour cream.

YOGURT CRAPPIES

4 TO 6 SERVINGS

EGG WASH:

2 eggs

2 tablespoons (30 ml) milk

1 teaspoon (5 ml) vegetable oil

1½ pounds (680 g) boneless, skinless crappie fillets

1 cup (140 g) seasoned flour (page 54)

¼ cup (55 g/half of a stick) butter

2 tablespoons (30 ml) vegetable oil

¼ cup (60 ml) plain yogurt

1½ teaspoons (1.5 g) dried dill weed

Paprika for garnish

Heat oven to 375°F (190°C). In mixing bowl, combine egg-wash ingredients; beat well with fork. Rinse fillets; pat dry with paper towels. Dip fillets in egg wash, allowing excess to drip off. Dredge with seasoned flour. In large non-stick skillet, melt butter in oil over medium-high heat. Add fillets; cook until golden brown on both sides.

Transfer fillets to shallow baking dish. Top with yogurt; sprinkle with dill. Bake for 10 minutes; sprinkle with paprika before serving.

FISH RECIPES
16

Parmesan Walleye with Champagne Sauce

4 SERVINGS

Fine restaurants offer the ultimate dining experience. Whenever I encounter a special meal, I try to analyze every aspect of the dish, from the spices and herbs used to make the sauce to the way different flavors complement one another. Then I go home and try to re-create the meal in my own kitchen. This recipe came from my attempts to re-create the Champagne Shrimp served at The Landing, a local restaurant owned by Jeff and Melissa Garlie. The sauce is particularly good when poured over wild rice.

Boneless, skinless fillets from 2-pound (900 g) walleye, or equivalent of any light gamefish

Salt

3 eggs

¹/₂ cup (63 g) freshly grated Parmesan cheese

1 cup (140 g) all-purpose flour

1¹/₂ cups (65 g) fresh bread-crumbs (page 118)

3 to 4 tablespoons (45 to 55 g) clarified butter (page 118)

¹/₂ cup (1.2 dl) champagne or Asti Spumante

2 tablespoons (20 g) finely chopped shallot

1 teaspoon (.3 g) dried basil

1 cup (2.3 dl) heavy cream or crème fraîche (page 118)

White pepper

Rinse fillets; pat dry with paper towels. Season fillets to taste with salt. In mixing bowl, combine eggs and Parmesan cheese; beat well. Dredge fillets in flour. Dip into egg mixture, allowing excess to drip off. Coat with breadcrumbs. In large nonstick skillet, melt butter over medium heat. Add fillets; cook until golden brown on both sides. Meanwhile, prepare the sauce: In saucepan, combine champagne, shallot and basil. Heat to boiling over high heat; cook until reduced to 2 or 3 tablespoons (30 or 45 ml). Add cream; reduce heat and simmer for a few minutes.* Season sauce to taste with salt and pepper. Serve with fish.

> ***Flavoring Tip**
>
> *If you have some fresh basil leaves available, chop a few and add them to the sauce while the cream is simmering. This will provide another layer of flavor.*

Mexican Walleye

4 to 6 servings

1½ to 2 pounds (680 to 900 g) boneless, skinless walleye fillets

Salt and pepper

1 cup (140 g) seasoned flour (page 54)

¼ cup (60 ml) vegetable oil

1 cup (2.3 dl) green chile salsa

2 cups (220 g) shredded Monterey Jack cheese

Sour cream for garnish

Heat oven to 350°F (175°C). Rinse fillets; pat dry with paper towels. Season fillets with salt and pepper to taste; dredge in seasoned flour. In large nonstick skillet, heat oil over medium-high heat until shimmering. Add fillets; cook until golden brown on both sides.

Transfer to baking dish. Top with salsa; sprinkle cheese evenly over salsa. Bake until cheese melts, about 10 minutes. Top with sour cream before serving.

Beer-Batter Fish

Variable servings

This basic beer-batter mix makes enough for several pounds (1 to 1.25 kg) of fish; it's easy to whip up another batch if you have more fish to fry (and more hungry guests!).

Oil for deep-frying

1½ cups (210 g) buttermilk pancake mix

1 egg, lightly beaten

1 cup (2.3 dl) beer (our favorite is Miller High Life)

1 teaspoon (3.7 g) baking powder

Seasoning salt and garlic powder

Boneless, skinless fish fillets, cut into 1-inch (2.5-cm) chunks

All-purpose flour, seasoned to taste with salt and pepper

Fill deep-fryer with oil and begin heating. In large mixing bowl, combine pancake mix, egg, beer, baking powder, and seasoning salt and garlic powder to taste; stir to mix thoroughly. When oil is 350°F (175°C), dredge fish in seasoned flour, shaking off excess. Dip fish into beer batter, allowing excess to drip off. Fry battered fish in hot oil until golden brown.

Done-Just-Right Fish

Just-right fish is opaque and moist. The layers flake easily when tested with a fork. Underdone fish is transparent and watery. The flesh does not flake easily with a fork. Overdone fish is dry and hard when tested with a fork. The flesh has little taste.

Taco Fish

4 TO 6 SERVINGS

4 flour tortillas, torn into pieces

1 teaspoon (2.5 g) garlic powder

Salt and pepper

SALSA:

1 tomato

Half of a green bell pepper, seeded

1 green onion

Juice from half of a lemon

3 tablespoons (8 g) chopped cilantro

4 to 6 boneless, skinless fish fillets (4 to 6 ounces/115 to 170 g each)

1 or 2 eggs, lightly beaten

2 tablespoons (30 g) butter

2 tablespoons (30 ml) vegetable oil

In food processor or blender, chop tortillas into tiny pieces. Transfer to plastic food-storage bag. Add garlic powder, and salt and pepper to taste; shake to mix. Set aside. Wipe out food processor or blender; add all salsa ingredients and process to desired consistency. Transfer to serving bowl; set aside.

Pat fish dry; dip in egg, allowing excess to drip off. Add to plastic bag with chopped tortillas; shake to coat. In large skillet, melt butter in oil over medium heat. Add coated fish; fry until golden brown on both sides, 3 to 4 minutes per side. Serve fish with salsa.

APROXIMATE PAN-FRYING TIME FOR FISH

TYPE	SIZE	COOKING TIME 1ST SIDE	COOKING TIME 2ND SIDE
Whole	up to 1½ inches (3.8 cm) thick	3 to 5 minutes	2 to 5 minutes
Fillets	¼ inch (.6 cm) thick	3 minutes	1 to 2 minutes
	½ inch (1.25 cm) thick	3 minutes	1½ to 3 minutes
	¾ inch (1.9 cm) thick	5 minutes	1½ to 3½ minutes
	1 inch (2.5 cm) thick	5 minutes	2 to 4 minutes

Coconut Crappie

4 TO 6 SERVINGS

½ cup (70 g) all-purpose flour

¼ teaspoon (.7 g) ground ginger

Salt and pepper

3 egg whites

Boneless, skinless fillets from 6 to 8 crappies

1 cup (75 g) shredded coconut

Oil for frying

In mixing bowl, stir together flour, ginger, and salt and pepper to taste. In another bowl, beat egg whites until foamy. Dip fillets in flour mixture, then coat with egg whites. Pat coconut onto both sides of fillets. Heat about 1 inch (2.5 cm) of oil in large skillet over medium-high heat until very hot but not smoking. Add coated fillets; cook until golden brown on both sides, turning once.

CAJUN WALLEYE

4 SERVINGS

1½ pounds (680 g) boneless, skinless fish fillets

½ cup (80 g) cornmeal

½ cup (70 g) all-purpose flour

Cajun seasoning blend (purchased, or prepared from the recipe on page 13)

2 tablespoons (30 g) butter

2 tablespoons (30 ml) canola oil

Rinse fillets; pat dry with paper towels. In medium mixing bowl, combine cornmeal and flour, stirring to mix well. Season fillets with Cajun seasoning to taste; dredge in cornmeal mixture. In large skillet, melt butter in oil over medium heat. Add fillets; cook until golden brown on both sides.

CAJUN CATFISH

6 TO 8 SERVINGS

This spicy recipe is easy to make and gives your fish a unique taste.

4 eggs, lightly beaten

¼ cup (60 g/60 ml) prepared mustard

¼ cup (60 ml) Tabasco sauce (more or less to taste)

2 to 3 pounds (900 g to 1.36 kg) boneless, skinless catfish fillets

Vegetable oil for pan-frying

Italian-style breadcrumbs

In glass or ceramic mixing bowl, stir together eggs, mustard and Tabasco. Add catfish fillets, turning to coat. Cover and refrigerate for about 8 hours, turning fish once or twice. When you're ready to cook, heat about 1 inch (2.5 cm) of oil in large skillet over medium-high heat until very hot but not smoking. Dredge marinated fish in breadcrumbs; fry until golden brown on both sides, turning once.

> TIMING
>
> *If the fillets are done before the rest of the meal is ready, don't despair. Just place the fillets on a plate, sprinkle them with dill weed and pop in a 190°F (88°C) oven for a few minutes while you finish the rest of the meal. Don't leave them in the oven too long, however, or they'll get soggy.*

CRACKER-CRUMB FISH

VARIABLE SERVINGS

Good-quality saltine crackers

Garlic salt

Lawry's seasoning salt

Lemon pepper

Eggs (1 egg will coat 1/2 to 3/4 pound/225 to 340 g fillets; use as many as you need)

Milk (use 2 tablespoons/30 ml milk per egg)

All-purpose flour

Boneless, skinless fish fillets (or skin-on, scaled fillets)

Butter*

Butter-flavored shortening*

Dried dill weed

Salt and pepper

Freshly squeezed lemon juice

Heat oven to 190°F (88°C). In food processor or blender, crush crackers into fine powder (or, place saltines in zipper-style plastic food storage bag and crush them with a rolling pin). You will need about 1/2 cup (35 g) of crumbs for each 1/2 to 3/4 pound (225 to 340 g) of fish. Place crumbs in large, flat bowl; season liberally with garlic salt, seasoning salt and lemon pepper. In another bowl, beat together egg(s) and milk. Place flour in flat dish. Rinse fillets; pat dry with paper towels. Dredge fillets in flour, shaking off excess. Dip into egg mixture, allowing excess to drip off. Coat with cracker crumbs.

In large nonstick skillet, melt equal parts butter and shortening. When mixture begins to sizzle, add fillets; cook until golden brown on both sides.

Transfer fillets to ovenproof plate; season liberally with dill. Place in oven for about 10 minutes (this allows the flavors to set, and gives you time to finish preparing the rest of the meal). Just before serving, sprinkle with salt and pepper to taste; drizzle with lemon juice.

*BUTTER SUBSTITUTION

If you prefer, you may use canola oil instead of the butter/shortening mix.

PECAN CATFISH

5 boneless, skinless catfish fillets (1/2 to 1 pound/225 to 454 g each)

Cajun seasoning blend (purchased, or prepared from the recipe on page 13)

2 eggs

1/2 cup (1.2 dl) milk

1 cup (140 g) all-purpose flour

3/8 cup (85 g/three-quarters of a stick) butter, divided

2 cups (213 g) chopped pecans, divided

Juice from 1 lemon

1 teaspoon (15 ml) commercial Cajun-style marinade

Season fish with Cajun seasoning to taste. In mixing bowl, beat together eggs and milk. Dredge fish in flour, shaking off excess. Dip into egg mixture, allowing excess to drip off. Dredge again in flour.

Melt 1/4 cup (55 g/half of a stick) butter in large skillet over medium heat. Add fillets; cook until golden brown on both sides. While fish is cooking, add 1 1/2 cups (160 g) of the pecans to blender or food processor. Add remaining 2 tablespoons (30 g) butter, the lemon juice and marinade; process until puréed.

When fish is nicely browned, spread pecan purée over fish; garnish with remaining 1/2 cup (53 g) of pecans. Serve immediately.

FISH CROQUETTES

2 1/2 cups (525 g) prepared mashed potatoes

1 cup (225 g) cooked, flaked fish (any kind)

1 egg, beaten

1/4 cup (25 g) chopped green onions

1/4 cup (15 g) chopped fresh parsley

1 teaspoon (2 g) Creole seasoning

2 tablespoons (15 g) all-purpose flour

Oil for frying

In large mixing bowl, stir potatoes with wooden spoon, smoothing any lumps. Add fish, egg, onions, parsley and seasoning. Mix well and shape into balls. Roll balls in flour and fry in hot oil until golden brown.

WALLEYE–WILD RICE CAKES

My friends know I never miss the opportunity to use wild rice in a recipe. One day I was experimenting with a new recipe for walleye cakes and decided to use some leftover wild rice in making the cakes. The results were so pleasing I added it to my recipe file.

8 ounces (225 g) boneless, skinless walleye fillets

1/2 cup (1.2 dl) white wine

1 cup (40 g) fresh breadcrumbs (page 118), approximate, divided

1/2 cup (75 g) cooked wild rice

2 eggs, beaten

1/4 cup (40 g) finely diced onion

2 tablespoons (20 g) finely diced green bell pepper

2 tablespoons (20 g) finely diced red bell pepper

2 tablespoons (30 g) mayonnaise

1 tablespoon (15 g) Dijon mustard

1 tablespoon (15 ml) Worcestershire sauce

A squirt of lemon juice

Salt and pepper

1/2 cup (110 g) clarified butter (page 118)

Heat oven to 400°F (205°C). In small glass baking dish, combine walleye and wine. Bake until fish just flakes, about 10 minutes. Remove from oven and crumble fish into large bowl. Add 1/2 cup (20 g) of the breadcrumbs, the wild rice, eggs, onion, green and red bell peppers, mayonnaise, mustard, Worcestershire sauce, lemon juice, and salt and pepper to taste; mix well with wooden spoon.

Use 1/2-cup (1.2-dl) measure to scoop up a portion of mixture, filling completely and packing tightly. Place portion on wax paper; flatten slightly with spatula. Repeat until all mixture has been formed into patties. Sprinkle generously with additional breadcrumbs. Turn with spatula; sprinkle second side with additional breadcrumbs. Cover with additional wax paper and refrigerate for 2 to 3 hours (this helps keep the cakes from crumbling while frying).

To finish the cakes, melt clarified butter in large nonstick skillet over medium-high heat. Add cakes; fry until golden brown on both sides.

CHOOSING A WINE

Today's shopper has at his or her disposal a wide variety of affordable wines that are ready to be used in recipes and enjoyed as a beverage along with the meal. Thanks to the proliferation of wineries in California, Washington, Oregon, Australia and elsewhere around the world, quality wines are now quite inexpensive.

FISH AND CRAB CAKES

A great appetizer can be the highlight of any meal, and this is one of my favorites. Fresh crab meat is best, but canned also works.

½ pound (225 g) fish fillets

1 tablespoon (10 g) diced red bell pepper

1 shallot, minced

1 teaspoon (3 g) minced garlic

1 mushroom, finely diced

3 tablespoons (45 ml) olive oil, divided

2 egg whites

½ pound (225 g) picked-over crab meat

¼ cup (28 g) fine cracker crumbs

¼ cup (15 g) chopped fresh parsley

1 tablespoon (15 g) Dijon mustard

Salt and pepper

2 cups (80 g) fresh breadcrumbs (page 118)

¼ cup (55 g) clarified butter (page 118)

Lemon-Butter Sauce (page 111)

Heat broiler. In saucepan, heat about 1 cup (2.3 dl) water over high heat until boiling. Place colander or sieve over saucepan. Add fish; cover and steam until fish flakes and is cooked through. Remove colander from saucepan and set aside to cool slightly. Pick off and discard any bones or skin from fish; flake cooked fish into mixing bowl. Set aside. In medium skillet, sauté bell pepper, shallot, garlic and mushroom in 2 tablespoons (30 ml) oil over medium heat until vegetables are soft, stirring occasionally. Remove from heat and set aside.

In large mixing bowl, beat egg whites with whisk or electric beater until foamy but not stiff. Add flaked fish, cooked vegetables, crab meat, cracker crumbs, parsley, mustard, and salt and pepper to taste. Mix thoroughly with wooden spoon.

Spread breadcrumbs on baking sheet; moisten with remaining 1 tablespoon (15 ml) oil. Broil crumbs until golden, stirring frequently. Transfer to flat dish. Shape fish mixture into balls the size of golf balls, packing tightly; flatten into patties. Press patties into breadcrumbs on both sides; transfer to plate lined with wax paper. Cover and refrigerate for at least 2 hours, or as long as overnight.

When ready to cook; heat oven to 190°F (88°C). Melt butter in large nonstick skillet over medium heat. Add crab cakes; cook until golden brown on both sides, turning gently to avoid breaking them up. Place finished cakes in oven while you prepare Lemon-Butter Sauce. Serve cakes with sauce.

ELIMINATING ODORS

To eliminate leftover cooking odors, try heating some ground cinnamon in a sauté pan over low heat. Shake the pan every now and then. The aroma will quickly permeate the kitchen.

Fish Cakes

This recipe is great with just about any type of freshwater gamefish, especially when served with one of the lemon sauces in this book (see page 111). It's a wonderful appetizer that also can be served as a main dish.

1 pound (454 g) boneless, skinless fish fillets

1 cup (2.3 dl) dry white wine

3/4 cup (30 g) fresh breadcrumbs*

1/2 cup (80 g) chopped shallots

2 tablespoons (20 g) minced green bell pepper

2 tablespoons (20 g) minced red bell pepper

2 tablespoons (30 g) mayonnaise

1 tablespoon (10 g) chopped pimiento, optional

1 tablespoon (15 g) Dijon mustard

1 tablespoon (1 g) dried parsley flakes

1 teaspoon (5 ml) Worcestershire sauce

1 teaspoon (2 g) Old Bay Seasoning

A dash of lemon juice

Salt and pepper

3 cups (285 g) cornflake crumbs

Clarified butter (page 118) for frying

Dried dill weed

Lemon-Butter Sauce (page 111) or Lemon-Dill Sauce (page 111), optional

Heat oven to 190°F (88°C). Place fish in glass baking dish; pour wine over. Bake until fish is just cooked through, about 10 minutes. Use slotted spoon to transfer fish to large mixing bowl; measure 2 tablespoons (30 ml) poaching liquid from baking dish and add to mixing bowl with fish. Add breadcrumbs, shallots, green and red bell pepper, mayonnaise, pimiento, mustard, parsley, Worcestershire sauce, Old Bay Seasoning, lemon juice, and salt and pepper to taste. Blend thoroughly with wooden spoon. Use 1/2-cup (1.2-dl) measure to scoop up a portion of mixture, filling completely and packing tightly. Place portion on wax paper; flatten slightly with spatula. Repeat until all mixture has been formed into patties.

Place cornflake crumbs in flat dish. Use spatula to carefully lift patties from wax paper; coat thoroughly with cornflake crumbs. In nonstick skillet, fry patties in clarified butter over medium-high heat until both sides are golden brown. Sprinkle with dried dill and place in the oven while you prepare the sauce. If you're not serving with a sauce, leave the cakes in the oven for at least 5 minutes to allow the flavors to set.

> ***Breadcrumb Tip**
>
> **When you grind the breadcrumbs, make a few extra. If the cakes are too wet, add enough breadcrumbs so they hold together.*

Oven-Crispy Walleye

4 TO 6 SERVINGS

Butter for greasing baking dish

6 boneless, skinless walleye fillets (about 6 ounces/170 g each)

Garlic powder, salt and pepper

¼ cup (55 g/half of a stick) butter, softened

¼ cup (15 g) chopped fresh parsley

1 egg

¼ cup (60 ml) milk

¾ cup (30 g) fresh breadcrumbs (page 118)

½ cup (63 g) finely grated Parmesan cheese

Heat oven to 450°F (230°C). Butter baking dish large enough to hold fish fillets in single layer; set aside.

Rinse fillets; pat dry with paper towels. Sprinkle with garlic powder, salt and pepper to taste.

In mixing bowl, blend together butter and parsley. In another bowl, beat egg and milk together with fork. In a third bowl, stir together breadcrumbs and Parmesan cheese. Spread butter-parsley mixture over fish fillets. Dip fillets into egg mixture, allowing excess to drip off. Coat with breadcrumb mixture. Place fish in prepared baking dish. Bake until fish flakes and breading is golden brown.

Spinach-Stuffed Fish Rolls

4 SERVINGS

4 boneless, skinless fish fillets (about 6 ounces/170 g each)

8 ounces (225 g) spinach, chopped, blanched and drained

¼ cup (30 g) grated Parmesan cheese

¼ cup (40 g) chopped onion

¼ teaspoon (1.2 ml) Tabasco sauce

2 tablespoons (30 g) butter

1 small clove garlic, minced

Paprika

Hot cooked brown rice

Heat oven to 350°F (175°C). Rinse fillets; pat dry with paper towels.

In mixing bowl, combine spinach, Parmesan cheese, onion and Tabasco sauce; mix well. Spread evenly over fillets; roll fillets around filling, jelly-roll style. Arrange fillets on nonstick baking sheet.

In small saucepan, melt butter over medium heat. Remove from heat; stir in garlic. Brush garlic butter over fish rolls; sprinkle generously with paprika. Bake until fish flakes, 20 to 30 minutes. Serve with brown rice.

FISH IN WINE SAUCE

6 SERVINGS

This is our own adaptation of a classic French recipe. It was intended for sole or flounder, but works very well with walleye and would be good with any dry, delicately flavored white fish. It works best with larger fish (3- to 4-pounders/1.36 to 1.8 kg). This elegant dish could easily be overpowered, and is best served with rice or boiled potatoes. Chardonnay or Riesling are good wine choices to accompany this dish.*

Butter for greasing baking dish

2 pounds (900 g) boneless, skinless fish fillets*

Salt and pepper

2 tablespoons (20 g) finely chopped shallot

5 tablespoons (75 g/half of a stick plus 1 tablespoon) cold butter, divided

1½ cups (3.5 dl) cold fish stock (page 11) or "emergency" fish stock (page 11)

2 cups (160 g) chopped mushrooms

½ cup (1.2 dl) white wine

3 tablespoons (45 g) softened butter

2 tablespoons plus 1½ teaspoons (20 g) all-purpose flour

½ cup (1.2 dl) heavy cream, or a bit more as needed

A squirt of lemon juice

⅓ cup (37 g) shredded Swiss cheese

1 tablespoon (3.5 g) chopped fresh dill weed, or 1 teaspoon (1 g) dried

Heat oven to 350°F (175°C). Butter a flame-proof glass baking dish. Rinse fillets and pat dry with paper towels; arrange in prepared baking dish. Season with salt and pepper to taste. Sprinkle shallots over fish. Cut 2 tablespoons (30 g) of the cold butter into small pieces; scatter over fish. Pour stock around fish; set dish aside.

In large skillet, melt 2 tablespoons (30 g) of the cold butter over medium heat. Add mushrooms; sauté until softened, stirring frequently. Spread mushrooms evenly over fish. Cover baking dish with kitchen parchment paper and place over medium heat. Simmer for a few minutes (be careful not to ignite the parchment). Transfer to oven and bake for 10 to 12 minutes, or until fish flakes. Carefully drain off poaching liquid (a bulb baster works well for this) and transfer to saucepan; set baking dish with fish aside. Turn on oven's broiler.

Add wine to saucepan with poaching liquid. Heat to boiling over high heat and cook until reduced to 1 cup (2.3 dl); meanwhile, blend 3 tablespoons (45 g) softened butter with flour to make a paste. When poaching liquid has reduced, remove from heat; stir flour-butter paste into liquid, stirring until smooth. Add cream. Return sauce to boiling, adding more cream if the sauce becomes too thick. Season to taste with lemon juice, salt and pepper. Pour sauce over fish in baking dish. Top with cheese. Cut remaining tablespoon (15 g) of cold butter into small pieces and scatter over fish. Place dish under broiler for 2 or 3 minutes, or until cheese melts and is beginning to brown. Remove from oven; sprinkle with dill.

> ***FILLET PREPARATION TIP***
>
> *It's a good idea to remove the lateral line (the dark meat down the center of the fillet, on the skin side) from fish that are 3 pounds (1.36 kg) or larger.*

Halibut Stuffed with Crab Meat

6 SERVINGS

You say you went to Alaska and came home with several boxes of halibut? Maybe a neighbor or friend caught a big halibut and doesn't know what to do with it. We know the feeling. After one of the first trips Babe made to Alaska, he came home with this recipe and it quickly became one of our favorites.

¼ cup (40 g) chopped shallot

4 ounces (113 g) sliced mushrooms, fresh or canned

¼ cup plus 3 tablespoons (100 g) butter, divided

1 can (6 ounces/170 g) crab meat, drained

½ cup (110 g) cracker crumbs

2 tablespoons (8 g) chopped fresh parsley

Salt and white pepper

8 pieces halibut (4 to 6 ounces/ 113 to 170 g each)

3 tablespoons (22 g) all-purpose flour

1½ cups (3.5 dl) milk

½ cup (1.2 dl) white wine

1 cup (110 g) shredded Swiss cheese

Heat oven to 400°F (205°C). Lightly grease baking dish large enough to hold half the halibut in a single layer; set aside. In skillet, sauté shallot and mushrooms in ¼ cup (half of a stick; 55 g) of the butter over medium heat until soft, stirring frequently. Add crab meat, cracker crumbs, parsley, and salt and pepper to taste; mix thoroughly. Arrange 4 pieces halibut in prepared baking dish. Top with cracker-crumb mixture. Arrange remaining halibut pieces on top; set aside.

In small saucepan, melt remaining 3 tablespoons (45 g) butter over medium heat. Stirring constantly, sprinkle in flour; cook, stirring constantly, until mixture thickens. Stirring or whisking constantly, add milk and wine; cook until sauce thickens slightly. Add salt to taste. Pour sauce over fish. Bake, uncovered, for 25 minutes. Sprinkle with cheese; bake for 10 minutes longer.

Mushroom-Baked Fish

4 SERVINGS

1½ pounds (680 g) boneless, skinless fish fillets

½ cup (110 g/1 stick) butter

1 tablespoon (15 ml) lemon juice

Salt and pepper

⅓ cup (25 g) sliced mushrooms

2 tablespoons (20 g) finely chopped onion

Heat oven to 350°F (175°C). Rinse fillets; pat dry with paper towels.

In medium skillet, melt butter over medium heat. Remove from heat; stir in lemon juice, and salt and pepper to taste. Dip fillets in butter mixture, turning to coat. Arrange in shallow baking dish. Top with mushrooms and onion. Spoon remaining butter mixture over fillets. Bake for 15 to 20 minutes, or until fish flakes.

EASY OVEN CRAPPIES

4 TO 6 SERVINGS

This is a quick, easy recipe for crappie or just about any other freshwater gamefish.

Butter for greasing baking dish

1¹⁄₂ to 2 pounds (680 to 900 g) boneless, skinless crappie fillets

¹⁄₄ cup (40 g) cornmeal

¹⁄₄ cup (10 g) fresh breadcrumbs (page 118)

¹⁄₂ teaspoon (.2 g) dried parsley flakes

¹⁄₄ teaspoon (.5 g) paprika

1 egg

Heat oven to 350°F (175°C). Butter baking sheet; set aside. Rinse fillets; pat dry with paper towels. Cut fillets into 2-inch (5-cm) squares. In mixing bowl, combine cornmeal, breadcrumbs, parsley and paprika; mix well. In another bowl, beat egg with whisk until foamy but not stiff. Dip fish squares in egg, allowing excess to drip off. Coat with cornmeal mixture. Place fish on prepared baking sheet. Bake until fish flakes and breading is golden brown.

CRISPY STUFFED FISH

4 TO 6 SERVINGS

This recipe works well with the bigger freshwater gamefish. We've enjoyed it with walleye and northern pike, and suspect it would work well with bass or even catfish.

3 tablespoons (45 g) butter, plus additional for greasing baking dish

1/4 cup (40 g) finely chopped onion

1/4 cup (30 g) finely chopped celery

1 clove garlic, minced

1 cup (40 g) fresh breadcrumbs (page 118)

2 tablespoons (8 g) finely chopped fresh parsley

Fish stock (page 11) or chicken broth, approx. 1/4 cup (60 ml)

Freshly squeezed lemon juice

Salt and pepper

1 1/2 to 2 pounds (680 to 900 g) boneless, skinless fish fillets (cut larger fillets in half)

1 cup (28 g) cornflakes

3 tablespoons (45 g) melted butter, approximate

Mushroom-Cream Sauce (page 112)

USING FROZEN STOCK

To thaw fish stock, place it in a small bowl. Microwave 1 cup (240 ml) of the stock at 100% power for 2 to 3 minutes; 2 cups (480 ml) for 3 to 4 1/4 minutes, until it is mostly thawed, but still cool. Use a fork to break up any remaining frozen pieces. Let stand 5 minutes.

Heat oven to 300°F (150°C). Lightly butter bottom of glass baking dish large enough to hold half of the fish fillets in single layer; set aside. In sauté pan, melt 3 tablespoons (45 g) butter over medium heat. Add onion, celery and garlic; cook until vegetables are soft, stirring often. Transfer to large mixing bowl. Add breadcrumbs and parsley; stir with wooden spoon to mix. Add enough fish stock to moisten crumbs. Add lemon juice, salt and pepper to taste, mixing gently.

Rinse fillets; pat dry with paper towels. Arrange half of the fillets in prepared baking dish. Season to taste with salt, pepper and lemon juice. Pile breadcrumb mixture over fish, pressing down firmly. Top with remaining fillets. Crush cornflakes into mixing bowl; add enough melted butter to hold cornflake crumbs together. Scatter mixture evenly over fish. Bake until fish is cooked through and topping is crispy, 20 to 30 minutes. Serve with Mushroom-Cream Sauce.

BAKED WALLEYE

4 SERVINGS

4 boneless, skinless walleye fillets (about 6 ounces/ 170 g each)

6 to 8 tablespoons (85 to 110 g) butter, melted

1 tablespoon (15 ml) lemon juice

Garlic powder, salt and pepper

1/3 cup (25 g) sliced mushrooms

2 tablespoons (20 g) finely chopped onion

Heat oven to 350°F (175°C). Dip fillets in melted butter; place in shallow baking pan. Sprinkle with lemon juice, and garlic powder, salt and pepper to taste. Top fillets with mushrooms and onion; drizzle remaining butter over all. Bake for 15 to 20 minutes, or until fish flakes.

DELTA BAKED FISH

This recipe came from Beth Jones, wife of former Delta Waterfowl Foundation vice president Lloyd Jones. Delta is one of our favorite conservation organizations and this recipe is one of our favorite ways to prepare walleye or just about any light-meat gamefish.

1½ pounds (680 g) boneless, skinless fish fillets

Salt and pepper

3 tablespoons (45 g) melted butter, divided

1 tablespoon (15 ml) fresh lemon juice

1 tablespoon (15 g) Dijon mustard

1 tablespoon (1 g) dried parsley flakes

1½ cups (75 g) crushed Rice Chex or cornflakes

Lemon-Butter Sauce (page 111)

Heat oven to 350°F (175°C). Rinse fillets; pat dry with paper towels. Place fillets in 10 x 15-inch (25 x 38-cm) glass baking dish; season to taste with salt and pepper. In small bowl, blend together 2 tablespoons (30 g) melted butter with lemon juice, mustard and parsley; pour mixture evenly over fillets. Bake until fish begins to turn white, about 8 minutes.

Meanwhile, combine remaining 1 tablespoon (15 g) melted butter with crushed cereal in mixing bowl. When fish has turned white, spread cereal mixture over fish; return to oven and bake until fish flakes and topping is golden brown, about 10 minutes longer. Top fillets with Lemon-Butter Sauce before serving.

HIDDEN VALLEY FISH

This recipe was sent in by a reader of my syndicated newspaper column and it's pretty good. I experimented with an alternative to the ranch dressing mix with pleasing results. I substituted 1 tablespoon (15 ml) lemon juice and dried dill weed. Either way, sprinkle some dried dill over the fish 5 minutes before it's done. Fresh dill, if available, would yield even better results.

1 cup (227 g) sour cream

1 cup (255 g/2.3 dl) mayonnaise

1 package (1 ounce) dry Hidden Valley Ranch dressing mix

1½ to 2 pounds (680 to 900 g) boneless, skinless fish fillets

1 cup (95 g) cornflake crumbs

Heat oven to 350°F (175°C). In mixing bowl, combine sour cream, mayonnaise and dressing mix; stir to blend. Rinse fillets; pat dry with paper towels. Dip fillets in sour cream mixture; coat with cornflake crumbs.

Arrange coated fish in single layer in baking dish. Bake for 30 minutes, or until fish is just cooked through.

It's in the Bag

4 SERVINGS

1¹/₂ pounds (680 g) boneless, skinless fish fillets

¹/₂ cup (80 g) cornmeal

¹/₂ cup (70 g) all-purpose flour

1 teaspoon (2 g) lemon pepper

¹/₂ teaspoon (3 g) garlic salt

Salt and pepper

¹/₄ cup (55 g/half of a stick) butter, melted

1 cup (95 g) sliced almonds

Heat oven to 400°F (205°C). Rinse fillets; pat with paper towels so fish are moist but not wet. In plastic food-storage bag, combine cornmeal, flour, lemon pepper, garlic salt, and salt and pepper to taste; shake to mix thoroughly. Add fillets; shake to coat.

Place fillets in glass baking dish. Drizzle melted butter evenly over fillets; top with almonds. Bake until golden brown and cooked through, 10 to 15 minutes.

Fish Delight

4 TO 6 SERVINGS

4 boneless, skinless fish fillets (6 to 8 ounces/170 to 225 g each)

8 ounces (225 g) cream cheese, softened

1 cup (255 g/2.3 dl) Miracle Whip

Pepper and garlic salt

¹/₂ cup (80 g) chopped onion

1¹/₂ cups (150 g) shredded Swiss cheese

Heat oven to 350°F (175°C). Lightly grease baking dish large enough to hold fish fillets in single layer; set aside. Rinse fillets; pat dry with paper towels.

In mixing bowl, combine cream cheese, Miracle Whip, and pepper and garlic salt to taste; beat together with hand mixer or fork. Spread mixture over 1 side of fish fillets; place in prepared baking dish, topped side up. Sprinkle onion over fillets. Cover and bake until fish just flakes, 15 to 20 minutes. Uncover; sprinkle with cheese. Return to oven until cheese melts, about 5 minutes longer.

BAKED FISH WITH HONEY-LEMON SAUCE

4 TO 6 SERVINGS

1½ to 2 pounds (680 to 900 g) boneless, skinless fish fillets

2 tablespoons (30 ml) honey

Salt and pepper

¼ cup (40 g) diced onion

¼ cup (55 g/half of a stick) butter

¼ cup (60 ml) dry vermouth

¼ cup (60 ml) lemon juice

Heat oven to 450°F (230°C). Rinse fillets; pat dry with paper towels. Arrange fillets in glass baking dish. Brush fillets with honey; season with salt and pepper to taste. Top with onion.

In small saucepan, combine butter, vermouth and lemon juice. Heat over low heat until butter melts, stirring frequently; simmer for 3 to 4 minutes. Pour butter mixture over fish. Bake, uncovered, for 20 minutes. Reduce heat to 300°F (150°C); cover dish with foil and bake for 15 minutes longer.

THAI FISH

4 SERVINGS

4 boneless, skinless fish fillets (6 to 8 ounces/170 to 225 g each)

Lemon pepper

Chopped fresh dill weed

Salt

⅔ cup (160 ml) buttermilk

¼ cup plus 1 tablespoon (75 g) mayonnaise

1 tablespoon (5 g) purchased Thai seasoning blend

Heat oven to 400°F (205°C). Lightly grease glass baking dish large enough to hold fillets in single layer; set aside. Rinse fillets; pat dry with paper towels. Season fillets with lemon pepper, dill and salt to taste. Arrange in baking dish; bake until fish flakes.

Meanwhile, combine buttermilk, mayonnaise, Thai seasoning, and dill to taste; mix well. When fish is flaky, pour buttermilk sauce over fish; return to oven long enough to heat sauce. Serve immediately.

EASY BAKED FISH WITH MUSHROOM SAUCE

4 boneless, skinless fish fillets (4 to 6 ounces/115 to 170 g each)

1 small onion, chopped

4 ounces (113 g) fresh mushrooms, sliced

¼ cup plus 2 tablespoons (90 ml) water

3 tablespoons (45 g) butter

3 tablespoons (22 g) all-purpose flour

2 cups (4.6 dl) milk

1 tablespoon (5 g) seafood seasoning blend

Salt and pepper

Heat oven to 350°F (175°C). Place fish in single layer in baking dish; set aside. In skillet, cook onion and mushrooms with water over medium heat until not quite tender. Add butter, stirring until butter melts. Add flour, stirring constantly to prevent lumps. Add milk, stirring constantly. Heat to boiling, stirring constantly. Season to taste with seasoning blend, salt and pepper; pour over fish. Bake for 15 to 20 minutes, or until fish flakes.

THREE SIMPLE FLAVORED BUTTERS THAT ARE GOOD WITH BAKED FISH

In small bowl, combine 6 tablespoons (85 g) butter or margarine, softened, with one of the following:

Citrus Butter—¼ teaspoon (.5 g) grated orange, lemon or lime peel.

Lemon-Parsley Butter—1 tablespoon (4 g) snipped fresh parsley, ¼ teaspoon (1.2 ml) fresh lemon juice.

Dill Butter—⅛ teaspoon (.1 g) dried dill weed.

BAKED CRAPPIE DIVINE

6 boneless, skinless crappie fillets (2 to 3 ounces/60 to 85 g each)

½ cup (110 g/1 stick) butter, melted

Chopped fresh parsley

Cajun seasoning blend (purchased, or prepared from the recipe on page 13)

Freshly squeezed lemon juice

Heat oven to 400°F (205°C). Rinse fillets; pat dry with paper towels. Brush bottom of baking dish with some of the melted butter. Add crappie fillets, skin side down. Pour remaining melted butter over fillets.

Sprinkle with parsley and Cajun seasoning to taste. Bake until fish flakes, about 10 minutes. Sprinkle with lemon juice to taste.

Broiled Hunan Bass Fillets

3 tablespoons (45 ml) soy sauce (low sodium if you like)

1 tablespoon (6.5 g) finely chopped green onion (white and green parts)

2 teaspoons (10 ml) dark sesame oil

1 teaspoon (1.7 g) minced fresh gingerroot

1 clove garlic, minced

1/4 teaspoon (.4 g) hot red pepper flakes

1 pound (454 g) boneless, skinless bass fillets

Heat broiler; spray broiler rack with nonstick spray. In measuring cup or small bowl, combine soy sauce, onion, sesame oil, ginger-root, garlic and red pepper flakes; stir well.

Arrange fish on prepared broiler rack; brush with soy sauce mixture. Broil 4 to 5 inches (10 to 13 cm) from heat element for about 10 minutes, or until fish flakes easily.

Grilled Walleye

4 TO 6 SERVINGS

This recipe was provided by Beth Jones, the wife of our friend Lloyd Jones, the former vice president for the Delta Waterfowl Foundation.

1/4 cup (55 g/half of a stick) butter

1/2 teaspoon (.5 g) paprika

1/2 teaspoon (3 g) onion salt

1/4 teaspoon (.5 g) pepper

1 1/2 to 2 pounds (680 to 900 g) skin-on, scaled walleye fillets

Prepare charcoal or gas grill. In small saucepan, combine butter, paprika, onion salt and pepper. Heat over medium heat until butter melts, stirring to blend.

Rinse fillets; pat dry with paper towels. Place fillets, skin side down, on grate over prepared coals. Cook until fish flakes and skin is blackened, basting frequently with butter mixture; cooking time will depend on thickness of fillets.

CRAPPIE WITH SHRIMP DIP

6 TO 8 SERVINGS

These fillets cook quite quickly (usually just a few minutes); keep an eye on them and remove from the grill as soon as the fish begins to flake.

8 boneless, skinless crappie fillets (2 to 3 ounces/60 to 85 g each); or skin-on and scaled

Juice from 1 lemon

¹/₂ cup (115 g) sour cream-shrimp dip

3 green onions, chopped (white and green parts)

Prepare charcoal or gas grill. Tear off very large sheet of heavy-duty foil; fold in half, shiny side in. Spray 1 side of folded foil with non-stick cooking spray.

Lay fillets in single layer on center of foil; sprinkle lemon juice over fillets. Spread thin layer of shrimp dip over fillets; sprinkle with green onions. Roll-fold foil over fish; roll-fold ends in to seal tightly. Place on grate over prepared coals and cook until fish flakes.

> ### HOMEMADE SHRIMP DIP
>
> *If your grocer doesn't happen to carry shrimp dip, try this homemade recipe. It yields about ¹/₂ cup.*
>
> *¹/₂ cup (115 g) sour cream*
> *¹/₄ cup (58 g) mayonnaise*
> *¹/₄ (30 g) cup grated sharp or very sharp cheese*
> *2 ounces (60 g) cooked shrimp (fresh or frozen)*
>
> *Mix sour cream, mayonnaise and cheese well. Refrigerate several hours or overnight.*
>
> *In a food processor, blend mixture with half the cooked shrimp. Remove to bowl.*
>
> *Coarsely chop other half of shrimp and add to mixture.*

BBQ NORTHERN FILLETS

4 SERVINGS

1¹/₂ cups (3.5 dl) beer (1 standard-size can or bottle)

1 cup (2.3 dl) bottled barbecue sauce

Juice from 1 lemon

1¹/₂ teaspoons (3.7 g) garlic powder

4 boneless, skinless northern pike fillets (about 6 ounces/ 170 g each)

Prepare charcoal or gas grill. In mixing bowl, stir together beer, barbecue sauce, lemon juice and garlic powder. Place fish fillets on large sheet of heavy-duty foil; spoon half of the barbecue sauce mixture over fish.

Place on grate over prepared coals; cook for about 15 minutes or until fish flakes, spooning additional sauce over fish while cooking.

SUE'S FISH AND CHIPS

6 TO 8 SERVINGS

8 boneless, skinless fish fillets (4 to 6 ounces/115 to 170 g each)

Juice from half of a lemon

½ cup (110 g/1 stick) butter, cut into 8 pieces

¼ cup (30 g) slivered onion

1 can (4 ounces/113 g) small shrimp, drained

Salt and pepper

½ cup (38 g) crushed potato chips

Prepare charcoal or gas grill. Rinse fillets; pat dry with paper towels. Tear off 4 large pieces of foil (preferably heavy-duty). Place 2 fish fillets in center of each piece of foil. Spritz fillets with lemon juice. Divide butter, onion and shrimp evenly between the 4 batches; sprinkle each with salt and pepper to taste. Divide crushed potato chips evenly between the batches.

Roll-fold foil over fish; roll-fold ends in to seal tightly. Place on grate over prepared coals and cook until fish flakes, 10 to 15 minutes.

FAST CRAPPIE GUMBO

4 SERVINGS

¼ cup (55 g/half of a stick) butter

½ cup (80 g) chopped onion

1 small green bell pepper, seeded and chopped

½ cup (60 g) chopped celery

1 can (28 ounces/794 g) tomatoes, undrained

1 can (12 to 16 ounces/340 to 454 g) okra, undrained

1 cup (2.3 dl) water

¼ to ½ teaspoon (.4 to .9 g) hot red pepper flakes

¼ teaspoon (.4 g) dried thyme

Salt and pepper

1 pound (454 g) cooked crappie fillets, cut into small pieces

2 cups (316 g) hot cooked rice

In large saucepan, melt butter over medium heat. Add onion, green pepper and celery; sauté until tender. Add tomatoes, okra, water, pepper flakes, thyme, and salt and pepper to taste. Adjust heat and simmer for 15 minutes.

Add fish and cook for 10 minutes longer; fish should flake into smaller pieces. For each serving, spoon ½ cup (79 g) of rice into individual soup bowl; pour fish mixture over the rice.

CATFISH ITALIAN STYLE

4 TO 6 SERVINGS

1 pound (454 g) uncooked spaghetti

¾ cup (165 g/ 1½ sticks) butter

8 ounces (225 g) fresh mushrooms, sliced

1 medium clove garlic, minced

½ cup (1.2 dl) dry white wine or chicken broth

¼ cup (15 g) chopped fresh parsley

2 tablespoons (30 ml) lemon juice

Salt and pepper

1½ pounds (680 g) boneless, skinless catfish fillets, cut into bite-sized pieces

½ cup (63 g) grated Parmesan cheese

Begin cooking spaghetti according to package directions. While spaghetti is cooking, melt butter in large skillet over medium heat. Add mushrooms and garlic. Cook, stirring occasionally, for about 5 minutes. Add wine, parsley, lemon juice, and salt and pepper to taste. Cook for about 3 minutes, stirring occasionally. Add catfish; simmer, uncovered, until fish flakes.

Drain cooked spaghetti, and serve catfish mixture over spaghetti (the sauce will be thin); serve Parmesan cheese with spaghetti.

WARM FISH APPETIZER

6 TO 8 SERVINGS

½ cup (110 g/1 stick) butter

1 small bunch green onions, chopped

½ pound (225 g) shredded Swiss cheese

1 pint (4.6 dl) half-and-half

1 tablespoon (7.5 g) all-purpose flour

1 pound (454 g) cooked, flaked fish

1 tablespoon (15 ml) sherry

Salt and pepper

Chopped fresh parsley, or dried parsley flakes

Melba toast or crackers

In sauté pan, melt butter over medium heat. Add green onions; cook until soft, stirring occasionally. Add cheese, half-and-half and flour; cook, stirring frequently, until cheese melts.

Stir in fish, sherry, and salt and pepper to taste; add parsley to taste and cook for about 1 minute longer, stirring constantly. Serve warm, with Melba toast or crackers.

BASS DILL DIP

ABOUT 2 CUPS DIP

This is a great appetizer that's easy to make and works with many types of fish.

1⅓ cups (285 g) cottage cheese

3 tablespoons (45 ml) ranch salad dressing

3 tablespoons (45 ml) lemon juice

¼ teaspoon (.2 g) dried dill weed

1⅓ cups (293 g) finely flaked cooked bass

3 tablespoons (21 g) finely chopped almonds

½ teaspoon (4 g) minced pimientos

In blender or food processor, combine cottage cheese, ranch dressing, lemon juice and dill; process until smooth. Pour into mixing bowl; add cooked fish, almonds and pimientos, stirring to blend. Cover and refrigerate for 1½ hours before serving.

FISH PIZZA

Prepare this fish pizza just as you would a regular one. Serve with garlic toast or as an appetizer.

1 small pre-baked pizza crust

1 can (6 to 8 ounces/1.7 to 2.3 dl) pizza sauce

2 green onions, chopped (white and green parts)

1 cup (225 g) cooked, flaked fish (any kind)

1 can (4 ounces/113 g) small shrimp, drained

½ cup (35 g) sliced fresh mushrooms

¼ cup (35 g) thinly sliced black olives

1 cup (110 g) shredded mozzarella cheese

Heat oven to 400°F (205°C). Place crust on pizza pan; spread pizza sauce evenly over crust. Sprinkle onions, fish, shrimp, mushrooms, olives and cheese over sauce. Bake for 15 to 20 minutes, or until cheese is melted and golden brown.

FRESH FISH HASH

6 TO 8 SERVINGS

½ pound (225 g) sliced bacon

½ cup (75 g) chopped green bell pepper

Half of a medium onion, chopped

1 pound (454 g) frozen hash browns, thawed

2 pounds (900 g) cooked, flaked bass

Lemon pepper, garlic powder, chili powder, salt and pepper

In large skillet, cook bacon over medium heat until crisp, turning as needed. Drain on paper towels, reserving drippings; crumble bacon. Sauté green pepper and onion in reserved bacon drippings until soft. Use slotted spoon to transfer vegetables to bowl; set aside.

In same skillet, fry hash browns over medium heat until slightly browned. Add fish, sautéed vegetables and bacon to hash browns in skillet. Season to taste with lemon pepper, garlic powder, chili powder, salt and pepper. Cook until slightly brown.

Hot Northern Salad

Be sure to remove any bones from the pike when you're flaking it.

1½ pounds (680 g) cooked, flaked northern pike

1 medium green bell pepper, cored and finely chopped

4 hard-boiled eggs, peeled and sliced

1 can (8 ounces/225 g) sliced water chestnuts, drained

1 can (6 ounces/170 g) crab meat, drained

1 can (4 ounces/113 g) small shrimp, drained

1 cup (120 g) sliced celery

1 cup (255 g/2.3 dl) mayonnaise

½ cup (80 g) chopped onion

¼ cup (18 g) sliced mushrooms

Salt and pepper to taste

1 cup (110 g) breadcrumbs

½ cup (110 g/1 stick) butter, melted

Heat oven to 350°F (175°C). Grease 2-quart casserole dish; set aside. In large bowl, combine all ingredients except breadcrumbs and butter. Mix well; transfer to prepared casserole dish. Sprinkle with breadcrumbs; drizzle with butter. Bake for 30 minutes, or until hot.

Super-Chilling Fish

It's hard to keep fish fresh on long trips into the backcountry. You'll be lucky to keep them for more than 2 or 3 days on ordinary ice. But you can keep them for a full week by "super-chilling" them with a mixture of ice and salt. Because the ice-salt combination has a lower melting point, about 28°F (-2.2°C), the fish stay colder.

You can super-chill fillets, steaks or whole fish that have been gutted and gilled. Wrap the fish in aluminum foil or plastic wrap. Add 1 pound (454 g) of coarse ice cream salt to 20 pounds (9 kg) of crushed ice and stir thoroughly. If you need less of the salt-ice mixture, reduce the ingredients proportionately.

Place the wrapped fish on a 4-inch (10-cm) bed of the salt-ice. Add alternating layers of fish and salt-ice, finishing with a generous topping of the salt-ice mixture. Later, as the ice melts, drain the cooler and add more of the salt-ice.

Toasted Fish Appetizer

This is a great appetizer that is both quick and easy to make.

½ cup (110 g/1 stick) butter, softened

7 ounces (200 g) sharp cheddar cheese spread, softened

Cooked, flaked meat from 2 walleye fillets or 4 crappie fillets

6 English muffins, split

In mixing bowl, combine butter and cheese spread; stir to mix well. Add fish; stir to combine. Spread mixture onto English muffin halves. Bake in toaster oven or under broiler until golden brown.

CHAPTER THREE

BIG GAME
R E C I P E S

WITH INCREASING AVAILABILITY OF FARM-RAISED BIG GAME MEAT IN SOME SUPERMARKETS AND SPECIALTY SHOPS, GAME IS ON THE MENU MORE THAN EVER. ELEGANT GAME DINNERS COMMAND HIGH PRICES AT TRENDY RESTAURANTS.

And as the popularity of farm-raised game increases, many hunters find that the truly wild game they take in the field is appreciated even more. A meal of big game meat truly is a priceless treat.

Most of the recipes we've included work equally well for any big game meat—deer, caribou, elk, moose, antelope and so on.

The substitution chart in the Appendix (page 120) can be a starting point for new ideas. Mixing and matching big game meats with recipes can be loads of fun!

TIPS FOR PREPARING BIG GAME

• If cooked properly, big game meat is even tastier than choice beef. And because it's leaner than beef, it also has fewer calories.

• If fresh herbs are available, you can substitute them for the dried herbs listed; simply double the amount.

• When a recipe calls for wine, use a good table wine. If you prefer to make the recipes non-alcoholic, you can use broth or water instead.

• If you happen to have bear meat, remember that it is usually stronger, darker and coarser than other big game and is usually prepared with more seasoning than the recipe calls for.

FALL-OFF-THE-BONE VENISON POT ROAST

6 TO 8 SERVINGS

Bone-in or boneless venison roast (3 to 4 pounds/1.36 to 1.8 kg)

Montreal steak seasoning

2 tablespoons (30 ml) vegetable oil

2 cups (320 g) chopped white onion

1 large tomato, cored and sliced

2 cups plus 2 tablespoons (4.6 dl plus 30 ml) white wine, divided

½ cup (1.2 dl) venison stock (page 9)

3 bay leaves

1 teaspoon (.75 g) dried thyme

1 pound (454 g) baby carrots (or regular carrots, peeled and cut)

1 pound (454 g) baby red potatoes, peeled and cut in half

½ pound (225 g) small white onions

2 tablespoons (15 g) cornstarch

Salt and pepper

Chopped fresh parsley for garnish

Heat oven to 300°F (150°C). Cut away all silverskin from roast; season liberally with Montreal steak seasoning. In large, heavy-bottomed Dutch oven that has a tight-sealing lid, heat oil over medium-high heat. When oil is hot but not smoking, add roast and brown thoroughly on all sides. (Browning seals in the juices; taking a little extra time to make sure the sides and ends are seared is worth the effort.) When roast is properly seared, remove Dutch oven from stove and drain any excess oil. Add onion, tomato, 2 cups (4.6 dl) of the wine, the stock, bay leaves and thyme to Dutch oven; return to heat. When liquid comes to a full boil, cover Dutch oven and place in oven for 4 hours.

Remove from oven. Transfer roast to plate; set aside. Strain liquid into wire-mesh strainer set over large bowl, pressing on vegetables with wooden spoon to extract as much liquid as possible. Discard vegetables; return liquid to Dutch oven. Add carrots, potatoes and small onions to Dutch oven; return roast to Dutch oven.

Place Dutch oven on stove and heat to boiling over high heat. Cover and place in oven again; bake for 1 hour, or until vegetables are soft. Transfer roast to serving dish. Use slotted spoon to transfer vegetables to dish; cover and keep warm. Place Dutch oven on stove over medium heat; meanwhile, stir together remaining 2 tablespoons (30 ml) wine and the cornstarch in small bowl. When liquid boils, stir in enough of the cornstarch slurry to thicken the gravy. Season to taste with salt and pepper; sprinkle with parsley.

BACON-WRAPPED BACKSTRAP WITH BLACKBERRY SAUCE

Don't be deceived by the long name; this dish is easy and quick. The sauce takes a few minutes to prepare, but it's worth the effort. Serve with your favorite wild rice dish or mixed vegetables, and a glass of hearty red wine.

2 pounds (900 g) venison backstrap (loin)

Montreal steak seasoning

Salt and pepper

Thinly sliced bacon (about ½ pound/225 g)

1 tablespoon (15 ml) olive oil

¼ cup (40 g) finely chopped shallots

2 cups (4.6 dl) red wine (merlot, cabernet sauvignon or pinot noir all work well)

3 cups (6.9 dl) venison stock (page 9) or beef broth

2 cups (290 g) fresh or thawed frozen blackberries

Pinch of dried sage

Heat oven to 350°F (175°C). Season venison with Montreal seasoning, salt and pepper to taste. Wrap the meat completely with slices of bacon. Place in glass baking dish; bake, uncovered, until desired doneness (25 to 45 minutes).

While venison is baking, prepare sauce: In saucepan, heat oil over medium heat until warm. Add shallots; sauté until soft and lightly browned. Add wine; cook until reduced to about half. Add stock, blackberries and sage; cook until reduced to desired consistency. (The sauce doesn't have to reduce to a syrup-like consistency; it can be a bit on the runny side.) When sauce is ready, strain through wire-mesh strainer, pressing on blackberries to extract as much liquid as possible. Salt and pepper to taste.

To serve, pour small amounts of sauce on individual plates; slice backstrap diagonally and place several pieces over sauce.

SPICED ELK HEART

When we asked different conservation organizations to contribute recipes, we didn't expect to receive one for spiced elk heart, but that's what we got from our friends at the Rocky Mountain Elk Foundation (RMEF) in Montana. They swear it's not only unique, but delicious as well. This recipe was provided for RMEF by Suzette Horton of Idaho Falls, Idaho.

1 elk heart

1 quart (.95 l) hot water

⅓ cup (80 ml) vinegar

3 tablespoons (37 g) sugar

2 teaspoons (12 g) salt

3 bay leaves

18 whole cloves

¾ cup (85 g) sliced onion

1 tablespoon (6 g) lemon zest (grated lemon peel)

Combine all ingredients in slow cooker. Cover and cook on LOW for 12 hours. Serve hot or cold.

Finger-Licking Honey-Glazed Venison Ribs

4 SERVINGS

I'm betting this will quickly become a family favorite, even for folks who don't think they like venison ribs. It's fairly easy to make and works with ribs from deer, elk, moose or any big game animal. The key to this recipe is slow-cooking the ribs in a hearty venison stock. If you don't have the bones to make a homemade stock, reduced beef broth will work.

MARINADE:

3 cloves garlic, sliced

1 cup (220 g) brown sugar

1 cup (2.3 dl) honey

¼ cup (60 ml) white wine vinegar

¼ cup (60 ml) Worcestershire sauce

Juice from 1 orange

1 tablespoon (18 g) salt

1 tablespoon (6 g) pepper

Full rack of venison ribs, cut in pieces to fit roaster

2½ cups (5.8 dl) venison stock (page 9) or beef broth, divided

In small saucepan, combine all marinade ingredients. Cook over medium heat, stirring frequently, until sugar dissolves. Remove from heat and set aside until cool.

Place ribs in gallon-sized (3.8 l) zipper-style plastic food storage bag(s). Add marinade; squeeze out as much air as possible. Refrigerate for as long as 24 hours, turning occasionally.

When you're ready to cook the ribs, heat oven to 400°F (205°C). Remove ribs from plastic bag(s), reserve marinade, refrigerating until needed. Place ribs in large roasting pan, meat side down, and place in center of oven. Brown for about 15 minutes on each side. When ribs are browned, remove roasting pan from oven and reduce oven temperature to 200°F (93°C). Place ribs on platter; set aside. Place roaster over medium heat; add ½ cup (1.2 dl) stock to roaster, scraping with wooden spoon or spatula to loosen browned bits. Remove roaster from heat; mix in remaining 2 cups (4.6 dl) stock and return ribs to roasting pan. Cover and bake (at 200°F/93°C) for 2 hours.

Near the end of the 2 hours, pour reserved marinade into saucepan and cook over medium-high heat until reduced and thickened. Remove ribs from oven; increase oven temperature to 300°F (150°C). Drain off and discard stock from roaster. Baste ribs liberally with thickened marinade. Cover roaster; return ribs to oven and bake (at 300°F/150°C) for 1 hour longer, basting with roaster drippings every 15 minutes. Before serving, heat remaining marinade and pour over ribs.

Meat Care

When butchering, you may want to leave an extra outer layer of meat or a portion of the loin attached to the ribs.

Tarragon Venison Backstrap

4 TO 6 SERVINGS

This recipe came to us from Randy Schoeck, our friend from archery manufacturer Easton. Randy says this dish was a pleasant surprise that resulted from accidentally grabbing a bottle of tarragon leaves instead of basil flakes. This recipe is great with wild rice or new potatoes and a glass of merlot.

2 to 2½ pounds (.9 to 1.13 kg) venison backstrap (loin)

¼ to ½ pound (113 to 225 g) sliced bacon

¼ cup (55 g) butter

1 clove garlic, minced

1 shallot, chopped

6 whole peppercorns, any color

1 cup (2.3 dl) white wine or dry sherry

1 cup (2.3 dl) heavy cream

½ cup (35 g) sliced mushrooms

1 tablespoon (1 g) dried tarragon

Salt and pepper

Prepare charcoal or gas grill. Wrap backstrap with bacon, securing with wooden toothpicks. Place on grate over hot coals and cook until bacon has nearly burned off, turning several times.

While venison is grilling, prepare sauce: In heavy skillet, melt butter over medium heat. Add garlic, shallot and peppercorns. Cook, stirring frequently, until mixture begins to caramelize. Add wine; cook until reduced by half. Add cream, mushrooms, tarragon, and salt and pepper to taste. Reduce heat so mixture barely simmers; keep warm until venison is ready. To serve, slice venison and smother with sauce.

Snowbank Italian Game Roast

SERVINGS DEPEND ON SIZE OF ROAST(S)

It's not often anyone has to serve wild game to 50 guests, but that's the predicament I found myself facing at a recent office Christmas party. Because we're an outdoor company, I wanted to serve lots of game dishes. But there's only so much space in the oven and just a limited amount of time on the day of the party. The solution? I cooked some venison roasts two days ahead in a large electric roaster. I sliced the cooked meat and let it marinate in the cooking liquid for 48 hours. Because the refrigerator was full, I stored the roaster outside in a snowbank. The roasts I made had an Italian flavor, but you can use any seasoning you like. It isn't necessary to use an electric roaster; a Dutch oven or blue roaster will work just fine.

Bone-in or boneless venison roast(s)

Italian seasoning

Garlic salt

Beef broth or venison stock (page 9)

Heat electric roaster or oven to 175°F (80°C). Season roast(s) liberally with Italian seasoning and garlic salt (or use seasonings of your choice). Place roast(s) in roaster or Dutch oven; add enough broth to come about an inch up the sides. Cook for 6 to 7 hours. At the end of the cooking time, remove meat and slice as thinly as possible, returning slices to roaster with cooking juices. Refrigerate or, if it's cold enough, put roaster outside. When it's time to serve, re-heat for an hour or longer at 200°F (93°C). What could be simpler?

BIG GAME RECIPES
46

INCREDIBLY EASY VENISON POT ROAST

8 TO 12 SERVINGS

When your guests are enjoying this dish, don't tell them how easy it was to prepare. Rather, let them think you spent all day slaving over a hot stove. This dish goes well with garlic mashed potatoes and a fresh green vegetable.

2 tablespoons (30 ml) olive oil

3- to 5-pound (1.36- to 2.3-kg) venison roast

1 cup (2.3 dl) red wine

1 or 2 onions, sliced

1½ to 2 cups (3.5 to 4.6 dl) venison stock (page 9) or beef broth*

2 bay leaves

Rosemary and thyme, dried or fresh

A small amount of dark roux (page 118)

Salt and pepper

Heat oven to 300°F (150°C). In heavy-bottomed Dutch oven that has a tight-fitting lid, heat oil over medium-high heat until just beginning to smoke. Add roast; brown well on all sides. Transfer roast to plate; set aside. Add wine to Dutch oven, scraping to loosen browned bits. Cook until reduced to a few tablespoons (30 to 40 ml). Remove Dutch oven from heat; add a layer of onion slices, and enough stock to come about ½ inch (1.25 cm) up the sides. Place roast on top of onions. Add bay leaves, and rosemary and thyme to taste. Cover top of roast with a layer of sliced onions.

Return Dutch oven to stove, and heat until stock is boiling. Cover Dutch oven, and bake for 3 to 4 hours, checking occasionally and adding additional stock as needed. When roast is fork-tender, transfer to warm plate; cover with foil and set aside. Remove and discard bay leaves. Place Dutch oven on stove; heat liquid to boiling over medium-high heat. Stirring constantly, add roux, a bit at a time, until gravy thickens. Season with salt and pepper to taste. Slice roast, and serve with gravy.

*VENISON STOCK

A dark venison stock imparts the best flavor, but beef broth or enhanced beef broth also works.

BROWNING

Browning the meat is a key. Searing all sides thoroughly seals in the juices. Use tongs rather than a fork to turn the meat. A fork will release too many of the meat's juices.

Jim Zumbo's Ginger Elk

3 OR 4 SERVINGS

This recipe was provided by our friend Jim Zumbo, who is not only one of the greatest outdoor writers in the country but a wonderful wild game cook to boot.

1 pound (454 g) elk steak

2 onions, sliced

2 cloves garlic

1/3 cup (24 g) minced fresh gingerroot

3/4 cup (1.8 dl) soy sauce

1 teaspoon (4 g) sugar

1 tablespoon (15 ml) oil

6 slices fresh gingerroot

2 tablespoons (15 g) cornstarch

Slice steak against the grain and place in zipper-style plastic food storage bag. Add onions, garlic and minced gingerroot to bag. In measuring cup, stir together soy sauce and sugar; pour into bag with elk. Seal bag well and shake to combine. Refrigerate for 1 hour, turning bag occasionally.

When elk has marinated for 1 hour, drain off and discard most of the soy sauce; elk should be moist but not too wet. Set elk aside. In large skillet, heat oil over medium-high heat until hot but not smoking. Add gingerroot slices; cook, stirring frequently, until browned. Remove skillet from heat; pick out and discard gingerroot slices. Return skillet to heat. Add elk; sauté until meat loses pink color. Sprinkle cornstarch over elk in skillet; sauté for a few minutes longer, stirring constantly.

Butt Kickin' Barbecue

4 TO 6 SERVINGS

"I normally don't like cover sauces that eliminate the uniqueness of game meat, but this is a great way to prepare any kind of game." So wrote Randy Schoeck of Easton Archery, who provided this recipe. He suggests serving this over rice, noodles or slabs of bread. He adds, "Cold, cold beer is a must!"

2 pounds (900 g) cubed venison (moose, elk, deer, caribou)

2 tablespoons (30 ml) olive oil

Salt and pepper

1 cup (2.3 dl) catsup

1/3 cup (80 ml) red wine vinegar

1/4 cup (60 ml) Worcestershire sauce

1 large onion, diced

3 cloves garlic, minced

2 jalapeño peppers, minced

3/4 cup (165 g) brown sugar

In large skillet, brown venison on all sides in oil over medium-high heat. Remove from heat; season to taste with salt and pepper.

In Dutch oven or large, heavy skillet, combine catsup, vinegar, Worcestershire sauce, onion, garlic and peppers. Cook over medium heat, stirring constantly, until smooth. Sprinkle brown sugar into Dutch oven, stirring constantly; stir until smooth. Add browned meat; cover and simmer for about an hour "until everything is nice and friendly in the pot."

BARBECUE VENISON

I've tried a lot of barbecue recipes and this is one of the best. It works very well for ribs, but is also great with steaks and chops. You can make this dish using a commercial barbecue sauce, but it isn't as tasty as the homemade version. I prefer to serve this meal with one of the squash-potato or sweet potato-potato side dishes in the side-dish section (beginning on page 102).

Venison ribs, steaks or chops

2 cups (4.6 dl) venison stock (page 9) or beef broth

1 onion, sliced

2 bay leaves

6 whole black peppercorns

Salt and pepper

SAUCE:

2 cups (4.6 dl) catsup

1 cup (2.3 dl) cider vinegar

1 cup (2.3 dl) pineapple juice (fresh or canned)

3/4 cup (1.8 dl) honey

1/4 cup (60 ml) soy sauce

1/4 cup (60 ml) Worcestershire sauce

1 teaspoon (.3 g) dried oregano

1 teaspoon (.75 g) dried thyme

1/2 teaspoon (.9 g) hot red pepper flakes

2 cloves garlic, minced

Heat oven to 250°F (120°C). In roasting pan or large nonstick skillet, combine venison, stock, onion, bay leaves, peppercorns, and salt and pepper to taste. Heat to boiling over medium-high heat, then boil gently for 5 minutes. Cover; place in oven and bake while you prepare the sauce.

While venison is baking, prepare the sauce: In skillet, combine all sauce ingredients. Heat to boiling over high heat, stirring constantly. Reduce heat to simmer and cook for 1 hour, stirring occasionally.

Near the end of the hour, prepare charcoal or gas grill. Remove venison from roasting pan. Coat thoroughly with sauce; grill for 10 to 15 minutes, or as desired.

SPICES & HERBS

Use dried spices and herbs carefully. Remember that they have shelf lives of only six months or so; beyond that point, they begin to lose their flavor. If you are not sure of the flavor of a spice, add less than recommended at first. It's always easy to add more, but impossible to remove what's already added.

BIG GAME CHISLIC

4 TO 6 SERVINGS

In all my travels, I've run across the dish called "chislic" only in South Dakota. Chislic is nothing more than deep-fried chunks of meat, and it's found on the appetizer menus of bars and restaurants all across the state. I decided to give it a try with venison and it was a big hit. It can be prepared with any big game, and it's quick and easy to make.

1 pound (454 g) venison steak or roast

Teriyaki sauce (or your favorite marinade)

Vegetable oil or canola oil for deep-frying

Barbecue sauce or dipping sauce for serving

Cut venison into bite-size chunks; place in glass or ceramic bowl. Add teriyaki sauce to just cover, stirring to coat. Cover and refrigerate for 1 hour, stirring several times.

Heat 3 inches (7.5 cm) oil in deep-fryer or deep pot until a wooden chopstick or toothpick bubbles when held in the hot oil. Drain venison chunks and fry, a few at a time, in hot oil. Place on paper towel to absorb excess grease. Serve with barbecue sauce.

GOVERNOR'S VENISON RECIPE

6 TO 8 SERVINGS

Jesse Ventura, the former governor of Minnesota, once told an interviewer that one of the biggest perks of his job was having his own chefs. Because Minnesota is such an outdoor state, we figured those chefs might have some good game and fish recipes, and we were right. Chef Ken Grogg provided several recipes for this cookbook, including this one for "venison forestière." We tried it and liked it. We think you will, too.

3 pounds (1.36 kg) venison chops or steaks

Salt and pepper

2 tablespoons (30 ml) olive oil

3 cups (240 g) chopped mushrooms

2 tablespoons (30 g) butter

2 shallots, finely diced

2 cloves garlic, crushed

3 sprigs fresh thyme

¼ cup (60 ml) brandy

¼ cup (60 ml) red wine

3 cups (6.9 dl) venison stock (page 9) or beef broth

Heat oven to 350°F (175°C). Season venison with salt and pepper to taste. In large skillet, brown venison on all sides in oil over medium-high heat. Transfer browned venison to shallow baking dish; set aside. Add mushrooms, butter, shallots, garlic and thyme to skillet; reduce heat to medium and sauté until mushrooms are soft. Transfer mushroom mixture to bowl; set aside. Remove skillet from heat; add brandy, stirring to loosen any browned bits. Carefully ignite brandy with long-handled wooden match. When flames die down, add wine and set aside.

In saucepan, heat stock to boiling over high heat. Add brandy mixture to stock; boil until reduced to desired consistency. Meanwhile, place venison in oven and cook for about 10 minutes, or until desired doneness. When stock mixture is desired consistency, add mushroom mixture; season to taste with salt and pepper.

When venison is desired doneness, remove from oven. Transfer to warm plate; tent loosely with foil and let stand for 10 minutes. Serve venison with sauce.

FOILED VENISON CHOPS

2 SERVINGS PER FOIL PACKET

2 venison chops (about 6 ounces/170 g each)

2 teaspoons (10 ml) olive oil, approximate

18 x 18-inch (46 x 46-cm) or 12 x 18-inch (30 x 46-cm) piece of heavy-duty foil

2 potatoes, thinly sliced

1 green onion, thinly sliced

Half of a red bell pepper, thinly sliced

Half of a zucchini, thinly sliced

1 carrot, chopped

Spike seasoning blend

Salt and pepper

Prepare charcoal or gas grill. Brush chops with oil. Place in center of foil (shiny side up). Top chops with potatoes, onion, bell pepper, zucchini and carrot; season to taste with Spike, salt and pepper. Seal packet tightly, rolling up ends several times to seal. Place on grate over prepared coals for 20 to 25 minutes, depending on the thickness; turn packet several times, being careful not to puncture foil.

VENISON STROGANOFF

4 TO 6 SERVINGS

2 tablespoons (30 g) butter

2 pounds (900 g) venison
steak, cubed

1 medium onion, diced

8 ounces (225 g) mushrooms,
sliced

1 clove garlic, minced

2 cups (4.6 dl) milk

1 envelope (1 ounce/28 g)
onion soup mix

A small amount of dark roux
(page 118)

1 cup (227 g) sour cream

In large skillet, melt butter over medium heat. Add venison, onion, mushrooms and garlic; cook until meat is browned, stirring frequently. Remove from heat; set aside.

In another skillet, blend together milk and soup mix. Heat to boiling over medium-high heat. Stirring constantly, add roux, a bit at a time, until gravy thickens. Reduce heat to medium-low and stir in meat and sour cream. Cook until just warmed; do not boil.

VENISON RUMAKI

VARIABLE SERVINGS; MAKE AS MUCH AS YOU WISH

This is a great, easy-to-make appetizer.

Venison steak, well trimmed

Teriyaki sauce

Canned whole water chestnuts,
drained

Sliced bacon

Cut venison into chunks the size of water chestnuts. Place in mixing bowl; add teriyaki sauce to cover, stirring to combine. Cover and refrigerate for at least 1 hour; overnight is preferable.

When ready to cook, heat oven to 400°F (205°C). Lightly grease baking sheet; set aside. Drain venison, discarding marinade. Place a chunk of venison on each side of a water chestnut. Wrap in bacon, securing with wooden toothpick. Arrange on prepared baking sheet. Bake until bacon is crisp, about 20 minutes.

Sautéed Venison Steak in Peppercorn Sauce

4 SERVINGS

This recipe is very simple to prepare, and it turns ordinary venison steaks into a delicious meal. One of the keys to this recipe is a reduced stock; simply simmer 2 cans of beef broth over very low heat until reduced down to about a cup (2.3 dl). The more the broth reduces, the more flavorful it becomes.

4 venison steaks (about 6 ounces/170 g each)

1 tablespoon (15 g) butter

Half of a shallot, finely chopped

¼ cup (60 ml) Cognac

2 tablespoons (30 ml) port wine

¼ cup (60 ml) heavy cream

3 tablespoons (45 ml) reduced stock (see note at beginning of recipe)

1 tablespoon (3 g) dried whole green peppercorns

2 to 3 tablespoons (30 to 45 g) butter, cut into small pieces

A few drops red wine vinegar

Salt and pepper

Sautéed mushrooms for serving

Heat oven to 190°F (88°C). In heavy-bottomed skillet over medium-high heat, sauté venison steaks in butter until well seared but not cooked through. Transfer to warm plate and place in oven to keep warm. Drain off butter remaining in pan. Allow skillet to cool for a few minutes.

Add shallot to cooled skillet; stir briefly, then add Cognac and port. Cook over medium-high heat until most of the alcohol has burned off, about a minute. Reduce heat to medium; add cream, reduced stock and peppercorns. Cook until sauce reduces and thickens slightly; meanwhile, remove steaks from oven and set aside to allow the juices to equalize.* When sauce has thickened slightly, stir in butter, vinegar, and salt and pepper to taste.

To serve, transfer steaks to individual warmed plates. Cover with sautéed mushrooms; top with peppercorn sauce.

* Steak Tip

Steaks will continue to cook when you take them out of the oven. Letting the steaks rest for a few minutes before serving allows the juices to reabsorb into the meat rather than run all over the plate.

Turning Steaks

Always use tongs rather than a fork to turn steaks. Puncturing steak with a fork will allow the juices to escape.

VENISON STEW

6 SERVINGS

Here's a stick-to-your-ribs dish that is easy to make and tastes great.
Serve with baking powder biscuits.

SEASONED FLOUR:

1 cup (140 g) all-purpose flour

1 tablespoon (5 g) paprika

1 tablespoon (18 g) salt

1 tablespoon (6 g) freshly ground pepper

1 pound (454 g) venison, cut into bite-size pieces

1 tablespoon (15 ml) olive oil

1 large onion, quartered

2 large cloves garlic, minced

1 teaspoon (.75 g) dried thyme

1 quart (.95 l) venison stock (page 9) or beef broth, divided

2 cups (300 g) cut-up potatoes (bite-size pieces)

2 cups (255 g) cut-up carrots (bite-size pieces)

1/2 cup (35 g) sautéed mushrooms

1 cup (200 g) frozen peas

Cornstarch slurry: 1 cup (2.3 dl) white wine mixed with 1 tablespoon (8 g) cornstarch (may not be needed)

Salt and pepper

Heat oven to 300°F (150°C). Combine seasoned-flour ingredients in zipper-style plastic food storage bag; shake to mix. Add venison pieces; shake to coat.

Heat oil in Dutch oven over medium-high heat. Add floured venison pieces and brown on all sides, turning as necessary; while venison is browning, add onion, garlic and thyme to Dutch oven along with venison.

When venison is nicely browned, add 1/2 cup (1.2 dl) of the stock, stirring with wooden spoon to loosen browned bits on bottom of Dutch oven. When browned bits have been scraped loose, add remaining 3 1/2 cups (8.1 dl) stock. Heat to boiling, then cover tightly and place in oven. Bake for 2 hours.

After 2 hours, add potatoes and carrots to Dutch oven. Re-cover and bake for 30 minutes longer. Near the end of the 30 minutes, stir in sautéed mushrooms and peas. If gravy is not as thick as you'd like, stir in some of the cornstarch slurry and cook on stovetop until gravy thickens. Season to taste with salt and pepper.

HAVE SOME LEFTOVER STEW?

Leftover thick stew makes a great filling for split pita breads. It can also be used to make a game pie. Follow standard pie-making procedures, filling pie pastry-lined pie plate with leftover stew. Top with second pastry. Brush with beaten egg and bake at 375°F (190°C) until crust is golden brown.

Venison Meatballs

Looking for a great recipe for that ground venison in your freezer? You'll like this one. It works with any kind of ground venison. It goes great with Garlic-Herb Mashed Potatoes (page 104).

1 tablespoon (10 g) minced onion

3 tablespoons (45 g) butter, divided

1 cup (40 g) fresh breadcrumbs (page 118)

1 cup (2.3 dl) water

1¹⁄₂ pounds (680 g) ground venison

¹⁄₂ pound (225 g) ground pork

2 large egg yolks

¹⁄₄ teaspoon (1.5 g) seasoning salt

Salt and freshly ground pepper

2 cups (4.6 dl) venison stock (page 9) or beef broth

A small amount of dark roux (page 118)

In large skillet, sauté onion in 1 tablespoon (15 g) butter over medium heat until soft; remove from heat. In large bowl, blend breadcrumbs and water with electric mixer. Add onion, venison, pork, egg yolks, seasoning salt, and salt and pepper to taste. Beat at low speed until thoroughly mixed. Using spoon, form meat mixture into small balls.

Melt remaining 2 tablespoons (30 g) butter in large skillet; add meatballs and brown on all sides. Transfer to dish; set aside and keep warm. Add stock to same skillet; heat to simmering over medium heat. Stirring constantly, add roux, a bit at a time, until gravy thickens. Reduce heat to low. Add meatballs; cover and simmer for a few minutes, or until you're ready to serve them.

Venison-Wild Rice Soup

This recipe marries delicious wild rice with richly flavored ground venison. It's easy to make and is a real crowd-pleaser. Note: The venison is best if spiced with some sausage seasoning.

1 pound (454 g) ground venison (preferably seasoned with sausage seasoning)

1 cup (2.3 dl) whole milk

2 cans (10³⁄₄ ounces/305 g each) cream of potato soup

2 cups (300 g) cooked wild rice

1 carrot, grated

Salt and pepper

Dried sage, optional

In large skillet, brown venison over medium heat, stirring to break up. Drain and discard grease. In large saucepan, combine browned venison, milk, soup and wild rice. Heat over medium heat until just boiling. Add carrot; reduce heat and simmer for a few minutes. Season to taste with salt, pepper and sage.

Venison Enchiladas

6 to 8 servings

- 1 package (1 pound/454 g) flour tortillas
- Vegetable oil
- 4 cups (900 g) shredded cooked venison
- 4 ounces (113 g) canned diced chiles, drained
- 1 can (4¼ ounces/120 g) chopped black olives, drained
- 1 large tomato, chopped
- Half of a medium onion, chopped
- 2 jars (approx. 17.25 ounces/489 g each) red enchilada sauce
- 1½ cups (170 g) shredded cheddar cheese
- Guacamole and sour cream for garnish

Heat oven to 350°F (175°C). In skillet, soften tortillas over medium heat, one at a time, in a little oil. As each is softened, fill with venison, chiles, olives, tomato and onion; roll up and place in 9 x 13-inch (23 x 33-cm) baking dish. Repeat with remaining ingredients until all filling ingredients are used up. Top with enchilada sauce. Bake for 1¼ hours. Remove from oven; sprinkle cheese on top. Return to oven and bake for 15 minutes longer. Before serving, garnish with sour cream and guacamole.

Stuffed Elk Peppers

6 servings

- 6 medium-size green bell peppers
- 1½ pounds (680 g) ground elk
- 1 cup (158 g) cooked white rice
- ½ cup (80 g) finely chopped onion
- 1 clove garlic, minced
- ¼ teaspoon (1.5 g) seasoning salt
- Salt and pepper
- 1 can (10¾ ounces/305 g) condensed tomato soup
- ½ cup (1.2 dl) water
- 1½ cups (170 g) shredded cheddar cheese

Heat oven to 350°F (175°C). Lightly grease baking dish large enough to hold peppers; set aside. Cut tops off bell peppers; remove and discard seeds.

In mixing bowl, combine ground elk, rice, onion, garlic, seasoning salt, and salt and pepper to taste; mix gently but thoroughly. Pack mixture into peppers and place in prepared baking dish.

In bowl, stir together tomato soup and water; pour over peppers. Bake for 45 minutes. Top with cheese and return to oven until cheese is browned.

Barbecue Meatballs

6 TO 8 SERVINGS

Serve with crackers and cheese.

1 pound (454 g) ground venison*

½ pound (225 g) ground pork*

1 cup (40 g) fresh breadcrumbs (page 118)

¼ cup (40 g) chopped onion

2 eggs, lightly beaten

Pinch of sage

Chopped fresh parsley

Salt and pepper

¼ cup (55 g/half of a stick) butter

3 cups (6.9 dl) barbecue sauce, or the homemade barbecue sauce below

In mixing bowl, combine venison, pork, breadcrumbs, onion, eggs, sage, and parsley, salt and pepper to taste. Mix gently but thoroughly; shape into 1- to 1½-inch (2.5- to 3.8-cm) balls.

Melt butter in large skillet over medium heat. Add meatballs; brown on all sides. Use slotted spoon to transfer meatballs to paper towel–lined plate; set aside to drain. Warm barbecue sauce in sauté pan over medium heat. Add drained meatballs; cook for a few minutes, until meatballs are warmed through. Remove from heat and let stand until the flavor of the sauce has been absorbed into the meatballs.

*Mixing Pork into Venison

I like to use 1 pound (454 g) of ground venison mixed with ½ pound (225 g) of ground pork. If your venison is already mixed with pork, thaw 1½ to 2 pounds (680 to 900 g).

Homemade Barbecue Sauce

2 cups (4.6 dl) catsup

½ cup (1.2 dl) dry red wine

¼ cup (55 g) brown sugar

¼ cup (60 ml) pineapple juice

3 tablespoons (45 g) Dijon mustard

3 tablespoons (45 ml) Worcestershire sauce

1 tablespoon (15 ml) liquid smoke

1 tablespoon (15 ml) red wine vinegar

½ teaspoon (1 g) paprika

½ teaspoon (1.5 g) chili powder blend

Salt and pepper to taste

Combine all ingredients in a sauté pan. Heat over medium heat, stirring constantly, until sauce comes to a boil and is thoroughly mixed. Reduce heat and simmer for 10 minutes or more, stirring as necessary, until sauce thickens. Adjust seasonings to taste.

CHAPTER FOUR

UPLAND GAME

R E C I P E S

BECAUSE WILD UPLAND GAMEBIRD MEAT DIFFERS SOMEWHAT FROM ITS DOMESTIC COUNTERPARTS, DIFFERENT COOKING TECHNIQUES ARE REQUIRED.

Wild birds, for one thing, have much less fat. Also, on most upland birds, the breast meat is lighter in color than the leg or thigh meat. But on some, the breast is dark as well. Light meat dries out more quickly, and usually requires less cooking time than dark meat.

Turkey, pheasant, grouse and partridge can be roasted much like domestic birds of the same size. Most medium-size upland birds like pheasant, grouse and partridge can also be split and grilled, or cut up and fried or braised. Small upland birds like quail, dove and woodcock are often baked in a covered casserole with liquid to keep them moist.

Consult the substitution chart in the Appendix (page 121) if you don't happen to have the bird suggested in a particular recipe.

TIPS FOR PREPARING UPLAND GAME

• You can roast a whole wild turkey much as you would a domestic one, but you must baste it more often to keep the meat moist.

• Wild birds tend to have more flavor; the best recipes are those that do not cover up the natural taste.

• Here are some general serving sizes of common upland gamebirds: A wild turkey serves four to eight people, depending on its size. A pheasant serves two, and a pair of grouse serves three.

SEASONED FRIED QUAIL

6 TO 8 SERVINGS

This recipe was provided by our friends at Quail Unlimited in South Carolina.

MARINADE:

1 cup (2.3 dl) buttermilk

1 tablespoon (15 ml) Tabasco sauce

2 tablespoons (30 ml) Worcestershire sauce

1 teaspoon (.75 g) dried thyme

Salt and pepper to taste

8 whole quail (4 to 6 ounces/ 115 to 170 g each)

1¼ cups (175 g) all-purpose flour, divided

1 teaspoon (2 g) paprika

1 teaspoon (6 g) salt

1 teaspoon (2 g) cayenne pepper

½ teaspoon (1 g) black pepper

Vegetable oil for frying

½ cup (1.2 dl) chicken broth

2 cups (4.6 dl) milk

1 tablespoon (15 ml) Worcestershire sauce

Salt and pepper

In large mixing bowl, combine marinade ingredients. Butterfly quail by cutting along the backbone and opening up. Place in marinade; cover and refrigerate for 8 hours. After 8 hours, remove quail, reserving marinade. In mixing bowl, stir together 1 cup (140 g) flour, the paprika, salt, and cayenne and black peppers. Dredge quail in flour mixture. Dip floured quail into reserved marinade, then dredge with flour a second time. Discard marinade.

In large skillet, heat about ¼ inch (.6 cm) oil over medium-high heat. Add quail and brown well on both sides; this should take about 10 minutes. Drain off all but ¼ cup (60 ml) oil. Add broth to skillet. Reduce heat to medium; cover and cook for 15 minutes. Transfer quail to serving platter; set aside and keep warm.

Drain all but ¼ cup (60 ml) drippings from skillet. Stir remaining ¼ cup (35 g) flour into drippings in skillet. Reduce heat to low; cover and cook for 2 or 3 minutes. Uncover and add milk gradually, stirring constantly until smooth. Increase heat to medium and cook, stirring constantly, until gravy thickens and bubbles. Stir in Worcestershire sauce, and salt and pepper to taste. Serve gravy with quail.

DEEP-FRIED WILD TURKEY

6 TO 8 SERVINGS

While the thought of deep-frying a turkey would probably give your grandmother a heart attack, it is truly a wonderful way to fix the bird. After eating a turkey (wild or domestic) fried in oil, you may never go back to the oven-baked version. The drawback to deep-frying a turkey is that it requires a lot of special, and somewhat expensive, equipment: a propane burner, a 30-quart (28 l) stainless-steel pot, a propane tank, lots of oil and a special thermometer. The good news is that once you try turkey (or a variety of other birds) in a deep-fryer, you'll use it so much it will more than pay for itself.

Vegetable or peanut oil to cover turkey, typically 3 to 4 gallons* (11 to 15 l)

Whole dressed wild turkey (12 to 13 pounds/5.4 to 5.9 kg maximum), preferably skin-on

Commercial butter-flavored marinade, or 1 pound (454 g) melted butter

Put enough oil in 30-quart (28 l) pot to cover turkey; heat to 350°F (175°C). While oil is heating, use meat syringe to inject turkey with marinade or butter (you can purchase a commercial injector or pick up a livestock syringe from a veterinarian or at a retailer who deals in farm and ranch supplies). When injecting turkey, make as few holes as possible. Insert syringe into breast and pump several ounces into the spot. Refill syringe, put it into same hole but pointed a different direction, and inject several ounces into the second spot. Inject 3 to 5 ounces (90 to 150 ml) in each breast half, and 2 to 3 ounces (60 to 90 ml) in each leg and thigh.

When the oil reaches 350°F (175°C), place turkey in frying basket and very slowly lower it into the pot. It's important to keep oil temperature between 325°F and 350°F (163°C to 175°C).

Cooking time is approximately 3 1/2 minutes per pound (454 g) . When done, the skin should be brown and crisp and the meat should be moist and flavorful; meat should register 165°F (74°C) with instant-read thermometer. Allow turkey to rest for 15 minutes before carving, allowing the juices to be absorbed into the meat.

> ***HOW MUCH OIL IS ENOUGH?**
>
> *One way to know for sure how much oil you'll need is to place the turkey in the pot and pour in enough water to cover. Remove the bird and mark the high-water mark on the inside of the pot. When filling with oil, put in just enough to reach that spot.*

WILD TURKEY AND STUFFING

Be careful not to overcook, as turkey has a tendency to become dried out. When injecting the bird, make only one hole in each breast, moving the syringe around the breast without removing it. If you make too many holes, most of the butter will escape before it's cooked into the meat.

STUFFING:

1/4 cup (55 g/half of a stick) butter

1 small onion, chopped

3 ribs celery, chopped

2 cups (140 g) sliced fresh mushrooms

1 clove garlic, minced

1 package (6 ounces/170 g) croutons

1 cup (150 g) cooked wild rice

2 eggs, lightly beaten

1 cup (2.3 dl) turkey stock (page 8) or chicken broth, approximate

Sage, rosemary, thyme, salt and pepper

Whole dressed wild turkey, preferably skin-on

Salt

1/4 cup (55 g/half of a stick) butter, melted

Turkey stock (page 8) or chicken broth for roasting (2 to 3 cups/4.6 to 6.9 dl)

1/2 cup (1.2 dl) dry white wine

A small amount of roux (page 118)

Pepper

Heat oven to 325°F (163°C). To make the stuffing: In large skillet, melt butter over medium heat. Add onion, celery, mushrooms and garlic; sauté until vegetables are soft. Transfer to large mixing bowl. Add croutons, wild rice and eggs, stirring to combine. Add stock, stirring with wooden spoon, until stuffing reaches desired moistness. Season to taste with sage, rosemary, thyme, salt and pepper. Set aside.

Rinse turkey inside and out with cold water; pat dry. Season cavity with salt. Use meat syringe to inject melted butter into breast and thighs of turkey. Spoon stuffing into cavity.

Place in roaster large enough to accommodate turkey comfortably. Add enough stock to come about 1 inch (2.5 cm) up the sides of roaster. Cover with foil and bake until juices run clear and meat near thigh registers 165°F (74°C), about 10 minutes per pound (454 g); baking time will depend on the size of the bird. Remove foil near the end of the cooking time to brown the skin. When turkey is done, transfer to serving platter; cover with foil and set aside to rest while you prepare gravy.

To prepare gravy: Tilt roaster and use bulb baster to remove as much stock as you can without collecting any accumulated fat; transfer stock to bowl. Pour off and discard fat from roaster; place roaster on hot burner. Deglaze by adding wine, stirring with wooden spoon to loosen browned bits. Pour reserved stock into roaster; heat to boiling. Stirring constantly, add roux, a bit at a time, until gravy thickens to desired consistency. Season gravy to taste with salt and pepper.

Yogurt Gamebird with Cream Sauce

4 SERVINGS

1 cup (227 g) plain yogurt

1/4 cup (60 g) Dijon mustard

2 tablespoons (6.5 g) snipped fresh dill weed

1 cup (225 g) cracker or cornflake crumbs

1/4 cup (55 g/half of a stick) butter, melted

2 boneless, skinless pheasant breasts (5 to 6 ounces/142 to 170 g each), split in half

1/4 cup (60 ml) dry vermouth

1/4 cup (60 ml) pheasant stock (page 8) or chicken broth

2 tablespoons (30 g) butter

1 cup (2.3 dl) heavy cream

A little fresh lemon juice

Salt and pepper

Chopped fresh parsley for garnish

Heat oven to 350°F (175°C). In mixing bowl, combine yogurt, mustard and dill; stir to combine. Place cracker crumbs in flat dish. Use meat syringe to inject about 1 tablespoon (15 g) of the melted butter into each breast half. Dip each breast half in yogurt mixture, turning to coat. Dredge with cracker crumbs. Arrange coated breasts in nonstick baking dish. Bake for 25 minutes, or until cooked through.

Meanwhile, in skillet or sauté pan, combine vermouth, stock and butter. Heat to boiling over high heat; cook until reduced to syrupy consistency. Add cream; continue cooking until sauce begins to thicken. Add lemon juice, salt and pepper to taste. Serve sauce over cooked breasts, sprinkling with parsley.

Quail with Rice

3 OR 4 SERVINGS

6 whole quail (4 to 6 ounces/ 115 to 170 g each)

3 cups (450 g) cooked wild rice

1 can (10 3/4 ounces/305 g) cream of mushroom soup

1 1/2 cups (3.5 dl) cream

1 can (10 ounces/284 g) mushrooms, drained, juice reserved

1/4 teaspoon (1.5 g) garlic salt

1/4 teaspoon (1.5 g) celery salt

1 package (1 ounce/28 g) onion soup mix

Heat oven to 350°F (175°C). Place quail in glass baking dish. In mixing bowl, stir together rice, soup, cream, drained mushrooms, garlic salt and celery salt. Cover quail with rice mixture. Cover dish; bake for 1 hour. In small bowl, stir together onion soup mix and reserved mushroom juice. Pour soup mixture over rice and bake, uncovered, for 15 minutes longer, or until golden brown.

OUTPOST LODGE PHEASANT

6 TO 8 SERVINGS

This recipe comes from Tom and Jill Olson, owners of the Outpost Lodge on the shore of Lake Oahe near Pierre, South Dakota. We've enjoyed a number of trips to the Outpost Lodge, fishing for walleyes and hunting pheasants and waterfowl. Pierre is truly a sportsman's paradise. During one of our trips, Jill whipped up this pheasant recipe, and everyone raved about it.

4 bone-in pheasant breasts (8 to 10 ounces/225 to 285 g each), skinned and halved

2 cans (12 oz./1.2 dl each) 7-Up

1½ cups (210 g) all-purpose flour

Lawry's seasoning salt

Pepper

Vegetable oil or butter for frying, approx. 2 tablespoons (30 ml)

Garlic salt

Chicken bouillon granules

2 cans (10¾ ounces/305 g each) cream of mushroom soup

½ cup (1.2 dl) milk

In large mixing bowl, combine pheasant breasts and 7-Up. Cover and refrigerate for 2 hours.

Heat oven to 350°F (175°C). Drain breasts, discarding 7-Up. In large zipper-style plastic bag, combine flour with seasoning salt and pepper to taste; shake to mix. Add pheasant breasts, shaking to coat. In large skillet, brown breasts in oil over medium-high heat. Arrange browned breasts in baking dish; sprinkle with garlic salt and bouillon granules to taste. Cover with water; bake, uncovered, for 1 hour 15 minutes.

Near the end of this baking time, combine soup and milk in mixing bowl, stirring to blend. Pour soup mixture over breasts. Cover dish and bake for 1 hour longer.

PHEASANT CORDON BLEU CASSEROLE

4 TO 6 SERVINGS

2 or 3 boneless, skinless pheasant breasts (5 to 6 ounces/142 to 170 g each), split in half

5 thin slices ham (1 ounce/28 g each)

4 to 6 slices Swiss cheese (1 ounce/ 28 g each)

1 can (10¾ ounces/305 g) cream of chicken soup

2 cups (80 g) stuffing mix

½ cup (110 g/1 stick) butter, melted

Heat oven to 350°F (175°C). Lightly grease 9 x 13-inch (23 x 33-cm) baking dish. Arrange breast halves in baking dish. Top with ham, then Swiss cheese. In small bowl, blend together soup and half of a soup-can of water (swirl the water in soup can to clean out clinging soup mix from inside can). Pour soup mixture over cheese. Spread stuffing mix over the top. Drizzle melted butter evenly over stuffing. Bake for 1 hour.

PHEASANT FOREVER

4 SERVINGS

We named this dish Pheasant Forever because it's a variation on a recipe we got from our friend Joe Duggan of Pheasants Forever, the Minnesota-based conservation organization. It can be prepared either in a 275°F (135°C) oven or a slow cooker. Cornbread goes well with this dish. Or, place one breast half atop a bed of wild rice for each serving.

2 boneless, skinless pheasant breasts (5 to 6 ounces/142 to 170 g each), split in half

Lemon pepper

1 cup plus 2 tablespoons (155 g) all-purpose flour, divided

2 tablespoons (30 ml) olive oil

2 cups (140 g) morels or other mushrooms*

2 tablespoons (20 g) chopped shallot

1 clove garlic, minced

¼ cup (60 ml) dry white wine

1 pint (4.6 dl) heavy cream

2 tablespoons (30 g) unsalted butter

1 tablespoon (1 g) dried parsley flakes

Salt and white pepper

Sprinkle breast halves liberally on both sides with lemon pepper. Place on plate; cover and refrigerate for at least 1 hour.

When you're ready to cook, heat oven to 275°F (135°C) if cooking in chafing dish; otherwise, have a slow cooker ready. Set aside 2 tablespoons (15 g) of the flour; dredge pheasant breasts in remaining 1 cup (140 g) flour. In large skillet, heat oil over medium heat until shimmering. Add breast pieces; brown on both sides and transfer to glass chafing dish or slow cooker. Add mushrooms to skillet; sauté until juices are released. Transfer mushrooms to chafing dish or slow cooker. Add shallot and garlic to skillet; sauté for about 30 seconds, then add wine and cook for a few minutes, until the alcohol evaporates. Add cream; cook, stirring constantly, for about a minute. Hold wire-mesh strainer over chafing dish or slow cooker; pour cream mixture through strainer. Cover chafing dish and bake for 2 hours, or set slow cooker on LOW and cook for at least 3 hours.

Near the end of cooking time, melt butter in small saucepan over low heat. Stirring constantly, sprinkle in reserved 2 tablespoons (15 g) flour; cook, stirring constantly, until mixture thickens. Cool this roux for about 10 minutes, then stir into chafing dish or slow cooker for final 15 minutes of cooking time. Before serving, stir in parsley; season with salt and white pepper to taste. To serve, top each breast with a spoonful of the sauce.

> ***MUSHROOM SUBSTITUTION**
>
> *When they're in season, morel mushrooms are the best choice, but portabellas, criminis, chanterelles or any other mushroom will work; combinations of two or more types also work well.*

FISH TACOS: P. 16

BEER-BATTER FISH: P. 18

WALLEYE–WILD RICE CAKES: P. 23

FAST CRAPPIE GUMBO: P. 38

BACON-WRAPPED BACKSTRAP: P. 44

FOILED VENISON CHOPS: P. 51

SAUTÉED VENISON STEAK: P. 53

VENISON ENCHILADAS: P. 56

VENISON RUMAKI: P. 52
PHEASANT PHINGERS: P. 83

SEASONED FRIED QUAIL: P. 59

PHEASANT FOREVER: P. 64

PHEASANT WITH ASPARAGUS: P. 82

Pheasant Dinner Pie: p. 93

DUCK DELIGHTS: P. 97

BRAISED CANADA GOOSE: P. 98

MARINATED DUCK BREAST: P. 101

GAMEBIRD MARSALA

4 SERVINGS

This simple-to-make recipe is great, especially if you double the sauce and pour it over wild rice or Wild Rice and Mushroom Risotto (page 109). This recipe came from "Big Steve" Turiseva, travel coordinator for Babe Winkelman Productions. Marsala wine is a sweet Italian wine that can be found with the cooking wines at most liquor stores.

2 boneless, skinless pheasant or ruffed grouse breasts (5 to 6 ounces/142 to 170 g each), split in half

Salt and pepper

½ cup (70 g) all-purpose flour

5 tablespoons (75 g) butter, divided

2 tablespoons (30 ml) extra-virgin olive oil

1 cup (70 g) sliced fresh mushrooms

1 cup (2.3 dl) Marsala wine

½ cup (1.2 dl) heavy cream

A small amount of roux (page 118)

1 tablespoon (1 g) dried parsley flakes

Heat oven to 200°F (93°C). Place breast halves between layers of wax paper and pound gently with meat mallet. Season breasts with salt and pepper; dredge in flour, shaking off excess. Heat large, heavy-bottomed skillet over medium-high heat, then add 3 tablespoons (45 g) of the butter. Add breasts and brown well on both sides. Transfer browned breasts to oven-safe plate; keep warm in oven.

Add olive oil to same skillet and heat over medium-high heat. Add mushrooms; sauté until very well browned and almost crispy. Add Marsala; continue cooking until reduced by half. Add cream and reduce heat to medium-low. Stirring constantly, add roux, a bit at a time, until sauce thickens slightly. Add browned breasts to sauce; simmer for a few minutes, or until ready to serve. Just before serving, remove skillet from heat and stir in remaining 2 tablespoons (30 g) butter, the parsley, and salt and pepper to taste.

BAKED PHEASANT WITH ASPARAGUS AND BLEU CHEESE

4 SERVINGS

I love this recipe, and I don't just mean the meal. The actual recipe is great, as you'll see when you read it. It comes from Bob Musil, executive director of the Red Wing (Minnesota) Convention and Visitor's Bureau, and was provided by Curt Johnson of the Minnesota Department of Tourism. I'm going to run it pretty much as written by Musil.

2 boneless, skinless pheasant breasts (5 to 6 ounces/142 to 170 g each), split in half

1 cup (140 g) all-purpose flour, seasoned to taste with salt and pepper

Vegetable oil, about 1 tablespoon (15 ml)

1 can (10 3/4 ounces/305 g) cream of chicken soup

1 ounce (28 g) crumbled bleu cheese

1/4 cup (60 ml) white wine

1 pound (454 g) fresh asparagus spears, tough ends snapped off

Hot cooked brown rice

Heat oven to 350°F (175°C). Musil writes, "Uncork a bottle of white wine and pour yourself a glass, taking care to reserve at least 1/4 cup (60 ml) for the recipe.

"Dust pheasant pieces in flour and brown in an oiled skillet. Arrange pieces in glass baking dish. In a mixing bowl, combine the soup, bleu cheese and wine. Pour mixture over browned pheasant pieces. Pour yourself another glass of wine; you deserve it.

"Bake for approximately 50 minutes or until sauce is bubbly and remaining wine is gone. Remove from oven and arrange asparagus spears on top. Cover with foil and bake an additional 15 minutes, or until asparagus is tender when tested with a fork. Uncork another bottle of wine and serve dish with brown rice. Enjoy." Indeed.

UPLAND "SHORELUNCH"

VARIABLE SERVINGS

Has this ever happened to you? You've reached the end of a long, successful day of upland hunting. The game has been cleaned, the gear is stowed and it's time to go home. But it's a gorgeous evening—there's a colorful sunset building on the horizon and off in the distance a wolf or coyote is breaking into song. What's the rush? Why not drop the tailgate and enjoy the waning moments of the day with an upland "shorelunch"? All it takes is a propane stove, a cast-iron skillet and a few simple ingredients.

Start by cutting a bird or two into bite-size pieces and sprinkling them with Cajun seasoning. Fire up the stove and melt a stick of margarine. When the margarine is smoking hot, toss in the meat and brown quickly on all sides. Serve the bits with toothpicks and a dipping sauce, which can be made ahead of time. Simply combine equal parts Dijon mustard and honey, stir in some dill weed and you're good to go. If you prefer a hotter dipping sauce, add a little horseradish.

(There's Something Fishy About These) Pheasant Phingers

2 TO 4 SERVINGS

While thumbing through a cookbook years ago we ran across a fish recipe that used Parmesan cheese and cracker crumbs. We tried it, liked it and have been using it ever since. One night some guests suggested the same recipe might be good with pheasant. We tried it using strips of breast meat and the results were impressive. It works equally well with ruffed grouse and Hungarian partridge.

2 boneless, skinless pheasant breasts (5 to 6 ounces/142 to 170 g each), split in half

1 cup (140 g) all-purpose flour

Salt and pepper

3 cups (120 g) fresh breadcrumbs (page 118)

1 cup (125 g) freshly grated Parmesan cheese

2 large eggs, lightly beaten

½ cup (110 g) clarified butter (page 118)

Cut each breast half in half lengthwise; each breast half will yield 2 "fingers." Place flour in shallow dish; season to taste with salt and pepper. In another dish, stir together breadcrumbs and Parmesan cheese.

Dredge pheasant fingers in flour, shaking off excess. Dip into beaten egg, allowing excess to drip off. Coat with breadcrumb mixture. In large nonstick skillet, melt butter over medium-high heat. Add breaded pheasant fingers and cook until golden brown on each side.

GAMEBIRD ALFREDO

2 TO 4 SERVINGS

Pasta lovers will enjoy this recipe. I prefer to fix it with cheese-filled tortellini, which is available in the freezer section of most larger grocery stores, but any pasta will work. This recipe is excellent using the breast meat from any light-meat gamebird.

3/4 cup (165 g/1 1/2 sticks) butter, divided

2 cloves garlic, minced

2 boneless, skinless pheasant or other upland gamebird breasts (5 to 6 ounces/142 to 170 g each), split in half

2 packages (9 ounces/255 g each) refrigerated cheese tortellini

2 cups (180 g) broccoli florets

1 cup (2.3 dl) heavy cream

A small amount of roux (page 118)

1 cup (125 g) freshly grated Parmesan cheese

3 tablespoons (27 g) pine nuts

Garlic toast* to accompany

In large skillet, melt 1/4 cup (55 g/half of a stick) butter over medium heat. Add garlic; sauté for about 1 minute. Add pheasant breasts and brown thoroughly on both sides. When breasts have browned, reduce heat to low; cover skillet and cook until just cooked through. Meanwhile, cook tortellini according to package directions; drain and set aside. When pheasant is cooked, remove from heat and cut into bite-size pieces; set aside and keep warm.

In saucepan, heat about 1 cup (2.3 dl) water over high heat until boiling. Place colander or sieve over saucepan. Add broccoli; cover and steam until just beginning to soften. Remove colander from saucepan and set aside.

In another skillet, melt remaining 1/2 cup (110 g/1 stick) butter over medium heat. When melted, add cream. Increase heat to high and cook until cream boils. Stirring constantly, add roux, a bit at a time, until sauce thickens slightly. Remove sauce from heat. Stir in Parmesan cheese, pine nuts, drained tortellini, broccoli, cut-up pheasant, and salt and pepper to taste. Serve with garlic toast.

*GARLIC TOAST

To prepare a tasty garlic toast, cut a loaf of French bread into 1/2-inch (1.25-cm) slices. Melt 1 stick (110 g) of butter and stir in garlic salt or garlic juice to taste. Dredge bread slices in butter, place on a baking sheet and bake at 350°F (175°C) until browned on each side. Toast can be prepared ahead of time.

JEFF'S FABULOUS PHEASANT

4 SERVINGS

This is a variation on a recipe we got from Jeff Garlie, owner and chef at The Landing, a lakeside restaurant not far from where we live in the Brainerd lakes area. Jeff and his wife Melissa worked for years in the Minneapolis–St. Paul area before deciding to open their own business. Jeff specializes in wild game, and this is one of the best meals on his menu. This recipe takes a little time to prepare, but it's worth the effort, especially if you're entertaining. Serve with wild rice or garlic mashed potatoes and a good Riesling or Chardonnay wine.

SAUCE:

1 cup (2.3 dl) white wine

2 cloves garlic, minced

1 bay leaf

6 cracked peppercorns

1 pint (4.6 dl) heavy cream

2 cups (4.6 dl) pheasant stock (page 8) or chicken broth

A pinch of dried rosemary

A small amount of roux (page 118)

Salt and pepper

2 tablespoons (30 g) unsalted butter

8 ounces (225 g) mushrooms, thinly sliced

1 or 2 cloves garlic, minced

1 tablespoon (15 ml) brandy

2 tablespoons (30 g) unsalted butter, plus an additional 2 tablespoons (30 g) for injecting, optional

2 boneless, skinless pheasant breasts (5 to 6 ounces/142 to 170 g each), split in half*

1 cup (140 g) all-purpose flour, seasoned with salt and pepper to taste

Prepare the sauce: Combine wine, garlic, bay leaf and peppercorns in heavy-bottomed saucepan. Heat to boiling over medium-high heat; cook until reduced by half. Add cream, stock and rosemary; reduce heat and simmer for 1 hour. After 1 hour, add roux, a bit at a time and stirring constantly, until sauce thickens slightly. Add salt and pepper to taste; simmer for 20 minutes longer. Strain sauce, discarding solids. In sauté pan or skillet, melt butter over medium heat. Add mushrooms, garlic and brandy; cook until mushrooms are brown, stirring occasionally. Add mushroom mixture to sauce; set aside.

Heat oven to 200°F (93°C). In heavy-bottomed skillet, melt 2 tablespoons (30 g) butter over medium-high heat. Dredge pheasant breast halves in flour, then add to skillet and brown on both sides. Transfer to plate.

Add remaining 2 tablespoons (30 g) butter to skillet and melt, then use meat syringe to inject melted butter into each pheasant breast half (this is optional, but adds flavor and juiciness). Place pheasant in casserole dish. Pour sauce over pheasant; cover and bake for 2 hours.

> ***SAVE IT FOR STOCK**
>
> *Jeff uses the carcasses from the pheasants to make the stock used in the recipe; if you have stock in your freezer, just place the carcasses in plastic bags and freeze them for another time.*

STUFFED, BACON-WRAPPED GAMEBIRD WITH PORT-MUSHROOM SAUCE

4 SERVINGS

This delicious recipe works well with pheasant, ruffed grouse, quail, partridge or any light-meat upland game.

½ cup (80 g) chopped shallot

½ cup (60 g) chopped celery

1 clove garlic, chopped

2 tablespoons (30 g) butter

2 cups (80 g) crouton-style stuffing mix

A pinch of dried sage

Enough gamebird stock (page 8) or chicken broth to moisten stuffing, about ½ cup (1.2 dl)

1 tablespoon (15 ml) extra-virgin olive oil

12 slices bacon*

4 boneless, skinless grouse breasts (5 to 6 ounces/142 to 170 g each), split in half*

SAUCE:

2 tablespoons (30 g) butter

1 cup (80 g) chopped mushrooms

½ cup (1.2 dl) Cognac

½ cup (1.2 dl) port wine

1 cup (2.3 dl) gamebird stock (page 8) or chicken broth

Heat oven to 325°F (163°C). In small sauté pan, cook shallot, celery and garlic in butter over medium heat until vegetables are soft, stirring occasionally. Transfer to large mixing bowl. Add croutons, sage and enough stock to moisten stuffing; mix thoroughly.

Pour oil into large cast-iron skillet. Place 3 slices bacon on work surface; top with 1 breast half. Pat some stuffing onto breast half; top with second breast half. Press firmly together, then wrap bacon completely around the bundle (secure with wooden picks if you like, but remember to remove them before serving). Gently place wrapped bundle in skillet; repeat with remaining ingredients. Place skillet over medium heat and brown bundles on both sides, turning carefully. When bundles have browned, place skillet in oven and bake, uncovered, for 30 to 45 minutes, or until the bacon is crisp. Remove from oven, place bundles on a plate and allow to rest while you prepare sauce.

To prepare sauce: First drain off and discard bacon grease from skillet. Place skillet on medium-high heat; add butter and mushrooms. Cook, stirring occasionally, until mushrooms are well browned. Add Cognac and cook for a few minutes to allow alcohol to burn off (be alert while doing this, as the Cognac may ignite). Add port, and cook for a few minutes longer to allow alcohol to burn off. Continue cooking until liquid has reduced to thick syrup. Stir in stock; continue cooking until mixture reduces and begins to thicken. To serve, slice gamebird bundles in half (unless small). Pour port-mushroom sauce over bundles and serve immediately.

*ADJUSTMENT BASED ON THE TYPE OF GAMEBIRD

Depending on the bird species you use, you may need to adjust the amount of bacon and breast halves; quail breast halves, for example, would require only 2 slices of bacon per bundle, but you would probably serve 2 bundles per person rather than 1. Also, if you're using pheasant, you may wish to cut each breast half into 2 thinner pieces (by cutting parallel with your work surface).

BRAISED GAMEBIRD SUPRÈME

4 SERVINGS

This recipe takes its name from the delicious sauce served with it—sauce suprème. The sauce isn' t as difficult or time-consuming as it may appear and it' s well worth the effort. Garlic mashed potatoes are a wonderful accompaniment for this dish. The flavors of the bird, the sauce and the garlic potatoes are a perfect blend. You can even scoop a little of the sauce over the potatoes. A green vegetable like string beans or fresh peas completes the entrée. Serve with a chilled white wine like Chardonnay or Riesling.

2 boneless, skinless pheasant or smaller upland bird breasts (5 to 6 ounces/142 to 170 g each), split in half

1 cup (140 g) all-purpose flour, seasoned to taste with salt and pepper

¼ cup (55 g/half of a stick) butter

2 cups (4.6 dl) gamebird stock (page 8) or chicken broth

SAUCE:

2 cups (4.6 dl) gamebird stock (page 8) or chicken broth

3 tablespoons (45 g) butter

3 tablespoons (22 g) all-purpose flour

½ cup (1.2 dl) heavy cream

A squirt of lemon juice

Salt and pepper

Heat oven to 250°F (120°C). Place breast halves between sheets of wax paper; pound gently with meat mallet. Dredge in seasoned flour. In large skillet, melt butter over medium-high heat. Add floured breast halves; brown thoroughly on both sides.

Transfer breast halves to roaster or Dutch oven; add stock. Cover and braise in oven for 1½ hours. Transfer cooked breasts to plate; cover and refrigerate until it's time for final preparation.

To prepare sauce: In saucepan, begin heating stock over high heat. In another saucepan, combine butter and flour. Cook this roux over low heat, stirring constantly, until thoroughly blended and smooth. When stock is boiling, slowly pour into roux, stirring constantly. Heat to boiling; cook for 1 minute. Reduce heat and simmer for 30 minutes, stirring occasionally. (You are making a "mother sauce" called *sauce velouté*.) Carefully remove any skin that accumulates on the surface during the 30 minutes. When sauce has simmered for 30 minutes, add cream, lemon juice, and salt and pepper to taste. If sauce is prepared in advance, cover and refrigerate until it's time for final preparation.

About 30 minutes before serving, heat oven to 250°F (120°C). Combine sauce and cooked breasts in chafing dish or covered skillet; warm in oven for about 20 minutes, or until the rest of the meal is ready for the table.

CREAMY BRAISED UPLAND BIRD

4 SERVINGS

This recipe takes a little time to prepare, but it's worth the effort. The end result is a melt-in-your-mouth dish drenched in a delicious cream sauce. This recipe will work with pheasant, ruffed grouse or any of the light-meat gamebirds. It would also be delicious with rabbit.

2 tablespoons (30 ml) olive oil

2 boneless, skinless pheasant breasts (5 to 6 ounces/142 to 170 g each), split in half, or equivalent in grouse, partridge or quail

1 cup (140 g) all-purpose flour, seasoned to taste with salt and pepper

1½ cups (3.5 dl) white wine (sauvignon blanc is a good choice)

1 shallot, finely diced

2 bay leaves

6 whole black peppercorns

3 cups (6.9 dl/1½ pints) heavy cream

1 cup (2.3 dl) pheasant stock (page 8) or chicken broth

Dried rosemary or sage

1 tablespoon (15 g) butter

8 ounces (225 g) wild mushrooms

1 tablespoon (11 g) chopped garlic

2 tablespoons (30 ml) brandy

A small amount of roux (page 118)

In large cast-iron skillet, heat oil over medium heat until shimmering. Dredge breast halves in seasoned flour; add to skillet and brown on both sides. Transfer browned breast halves to plate; cover and refrigerate. Add wine, shallot, bay leaves and peppercorns to same skillet. Increase heat to medium-high and cook until reduced by half. Add cream, stock and rosemary or sage to taste; reduce heat and simmer for 1 hour.

While sauce is simmering, melt butter in sauté pan over medium heat. Add mushrooms and garlic; cook until mushrooms are soft, stirring occasionally. Add brandy; heat to boiling. Remove from heat and set aside until final assembly.

Heat oven to 250°F (120°C). When cream sauce has simmered for 1 hour, add roux, a bit at a time and stirring constantly, until sauce thickens slightly. Combine cream sauce and sautéed mushrooms in Dutch oven. Add browned breast halves, turning to coat and pushing down into sauce. Season to taste with salt, pepper and rosemary or sage. Cover and bake for 2 hours. Serve over a bed of wild rice or with garlic mashed potatoes and a glass of the same wine used in preparing the sauce.

GAMEBIRD TIPS

When using gamebirds, I like to separate the breast meat from the tenderloins on the underside of the breast. The tenderloins are the tastiest part of the bird. Here's a little tip: After you brown the meat, place it in the refrigerator while you work on the sauce. Before putting the ingredients in the oven, inject the meat with a small amount of melted butter using a livestock syringe, available at most veterinary stores.

"Stuffed" Stuffing

4 SERVINGS

This is a delicious way to prepare the meat from any light-meat gamebird, and even works well with rabbit. It's fairly easy to make, requiring a minimum of prep time. The idea behind this dish is to bake the meat inside a moist stuffing, which will add moisture and flavor to the meat. If you want to take a shortcut, eliminate the slow-cooking of the meat and simply place the browned meat in the stuffing mix and cook. But slow-cooking the meat in a good game stock prior to making the final dish definitely produces a moister, even-better-tasting dish, and the reserved stock makes better wild rice and a more flavorful stuffing and gravy.

2 boneless, skinless pheasant breasts (5 to 6 ounces/142 to 170 g each), split in half, or equivalent in grouse, partridge or quail

Lemon pepper

1 cup (140 g) all-purpose flour, seasoned to taste with salt and pepper

½ cup (110 g/1 stick) butter

2 cups (4.6 dl) gamebird stock (page 8) or chicken broth

STUFFING:

1 cup (180 g) uncooked wild rice

2 tablespoons (30 g) butter

1 cup (70 g) sliced mushrooms

½ cup (60 g) chopped celery

¼ cup (40 g) chopped onion

1 clove garlic, chopped

3 cups (120 g) unseasoned stuffing mix, or bread cut into small pieces

¼ cup (4 g) dried parsley flakes

1 tablespoon (1 g) dried sage

1 egg, well beaten

Heat oven to 225°F (107°C). Season breast halves generously with lemon pepper; pound seasoning in with meat mallet. Dredge breast halves in the flour mixture. In large cast-iron skillet, melt butter over medium-high heat. Add breast halves; brown well on both sides. Transfer breast halves to roasting pan; set skillet aside for later use. Add stock to roasting pan; cover tightly and bake for 2 hours.

Transfer breast halves to plate; cover and refrigerate while you prepare stuffing. Increase oven heat to 325°F (163°C). In sauté pan, combine 1½ (3.5 dl) cups juices from roasting pan with wild rice. Simmer over medium heat until rice "pops" completely. Remove from heat; set aside. In small skillet, melt butter over medium heat. Add mushrooms, celery, onion and garlic; sauté until vegetables are soft, stirring occasionally. Transfer to large mixing bowl. Add stuffing mix, parsley, sage and egg, stirring to combine. Add about 1 cup (2.3 dl) stock from the roasting pan, stirring with wooden spoon or mixing with your hands, until stuffing reaches desired moistness. (It's important to make the stuffing mix quite moist. If it seems dry, add a bit more stock, another egg or a small amount of water.)

Place half the stuffing in glass baking dish. Layer breast halves over stuffing, then top with remaining stuffing. Bake, uncovered, for 30 to 45 minutes, or until the stuffing is done.

Just before serving, heat same skillet used to brown breast halves. Pour in a little of the reserved stock from the roasting pan and use a spatula to scrape up the caramelized bits from the bottom of the pan. Stir in the remaining stock to make gravy. The gravy should thicken when the stock comes to a boil. If it doesn't, stir a tablespoon of cornstarch in a cup of white wine and add a little at a time until the gravy thickens. Season the gravy with salt and pepper and pour over the stuffing-game dish.

PHEASANT BUNDLES

6 SERVINGS

2 tablespoons (30 g) butter, plus additional for brushing pie crust

1 cup (175 g) diced uncooked pheasant breast meat

1 cup (80 g) diced mushrooms

1/2 cup (100 g) finely diced onion

1 large clove garlic, minced

1/4 cup (60 ml) white wine

Dried rosemary, salt and pepper

1/2 cup plus 1 tablespoon (1.33 dl) heavy cream, divided

1 teaspoon (5 ml) lemon juice

Packaged or homemade pie crust for single-crust pie

12 spinach leaves, blanched and patted dry, optional

SAUCE:

1/2 cup (1.2 dl) dry sherry

1 tablespoon (15 ml) balsamic vinegar

4 matchstick-size pieces of fresh gingerroot

1 cup (2.3 dl) heavy cream

Heat oven to 400°F (205°C). In large, heavy-bottomed skillet, melt 2 tablespoons (30 g) butter over medium heat. When butter stops foaming, add pheasant, mushrooms, onion and garlic. Sauté until pheasant is just cooked through. Deglaze pan with wine; season with rosemary, salt and pepper to taste. Continue cooking until wine has reduced by about half, then stir in 1/2 cup (1.2 dl) cream. Continue cooking until liquid has reduced to a few tablespoons. Transfer mixture to food processor fitted with metal blade (or use a blender). Purée until smooth. Add lemon juice and remaining 1 tablespoon (15 ml) cream; process briefly.

Place rolled-out pie crust on work surface; flatten slightly with rolling pin. Cut into 6 pie-shaped wedges. Melt a few tablespoons butter; brush each pie-crust wedge with melted butter. Place 2 spinach leaves (if using) on each wedge. Spoon pheasant mixture onto center of each wedge and fold corners to center. Seal edges by pressing with your fingers. Place bundles on nonstick baking sheet; brush with melted butter. Bake for 12 to 15 minutes, or until golden brown.

While bundles are baking, prepare sauce: Add sherry, vinegar and gingerroot to same skillet used to cook pheasant. Cook over medium heat until reduced to about half. Add cream; adjust heat so mixture simmers and cook until thickened slightly and reduced to about half. Strain sauce, discarding gingerroot. Serve sauce over pheasant bundles.

Gamebird-Wild Rice Soup

6 TO 8 SERVINGS

This great-tasting dish is a wonderful starter, but also hearty enough to serve as a complete meal, especially if served with crackers or baking powder biscuits. The secret to its flavor is slow-cooking the game in a good homemade stock. One of the nice things about this recipe is that it can be made utilizing scraps of meat that might otherwise go to waste. If you breast your gamebirds (pheasant, ruffed grouse, quail, partridge or whatever) you'll notice there are bits of meat remaining on the carcass. These include the meat around the wings and under the wishbone, the back meat, and slivers of meat along the breastbone. Trim these pieces of meat and save them in a freezer-weight plastic bag, adding to the bag until you have about a pound of meat. Or, just cut a couple of boneless breasts into bite-size pieces to prepare this dish.

1 pound (454 g) boneless, skinless gamebird meat, cut into small pieces

Lemon pepper, or all-purpose seasoning such as Spike

1 cup (140 g) all-purpose flour, seasoned to taste with salt and pepper

¼ cup (55 g/half of a stick) butter

2½ cups (5.8 dl) game stock (page 8) or chicken broth

1 cup (180 g) uncooked wild rice

1 cup (2.3 dl) half-and-half

2 cans (10¾ ounces/305 g each) cream of potato soup

1 carrot, grated

Heat oven to 225°F (107°C). Season gamebird meat liberally with lemon pepper. Toss meat with flour mixture, shaking off excess. Melt butter in large cast-iron skillet; add meat and cook until thoroughly browned. Transfer meat to roaster; set skillet with drippings aside. Add stock to roaster; cover and bake for 2 hours. Remove roaster from oven. Use slotted spoon to transfer cooked meat to bowl; cover and refrigerate.

Measure 2½ cups (5.8 dl) stock from roaster; add additional stock or water if necessary. In saucepan, combine 1½ cups (3.5 dl) of the stock with the rice. Cover and cook over medium heat until rice pops, 25 to 30 minutes.

When the rice is cooked, place cast-iron skillet that was used to brown meat over medium-high heat. Add ½ cup (1.2 dl) of the stock; stir to loosen any browned bits from skillet. Transfer mixture to large saucepan (or, continue cooking in cast-iron skillet if you prefer, although it may become very full and unwieldy). Add remaining ½ cup (1.2 dl) of the stock, the half-and-half, soup and carrot to saucepan (or skillet). Add cooked wild rice and meat to saucepan. Cook over medium heat until warmed through.

A LITTLE EXTRA

You can spice up this dish by adding sautéed onions or even a few sautéed mushrooms.

GAMEBIRD TETRAZZINI

4 TO 6 SERVINGS

Here's a quick, easy recipe that can be thrown together in minutes and tastes great. It works with pheasant, ruffed grouse or any of the delicately flavored gamebirds.

2 cups (280 g) cut-up cooked pheasant or other upland gamebird meat

½ pound (225 g) Velveeta cheese, cubed

7 ounces (200 g) thin spaghetti, cooked according to package directions

1 can (10¾ ounces/305 g) cream of mushroom soup

1 can (10¾ ounces/305 g) cream of chicken soup

1 cup (2.3 dl) gamebird stock (page 8) or chicken broth

1 cup (2.3 dl) milk

5 drops Tabasco sauce

¼ cup (30 g) freshly grated Parmesan cheese

Heat oven to 350°F (175°C). In large mixing bowl, combine gamebird, Velveeta cheese, spaghetti, mushroom and chicken soups, stock, milk and Tabasco; mix gently but thoroughly. Scrape mixture into 9 x 13-inch (23 x 33-cm) glass baking dish; top with Parmesan cheese. Bake for 45 minutes, or until bubbly.

MEXICAN WILD TURKEY

4 SERVINGS

This is a great recipe for using up leftover turkey.

¾ cup (1.8 dl) salsa

1 can (10¾ ounces/305 g) cream of mushroom soup

1 soup can of milk

¼ cup (40 g) chopped onion

¾ cup (165 g/1½ sticks) butter, melted

1 cup (115 g) grated cheddar cheese

1 cup (110 g) grated Monterey Jack cheese

6 large flour tortillas, torn into bite-size pieces

2½ cups (350 g) cut-up cooked turkey meat

Lightly grease medium casserole dish; set aside. In mixing bowl, combine salsa, soup, milk, onion and butter; stir to blend. In another bowl, stir together cheddar and Monterey Jack cheeses. Place one-third of the tortilla pieces into prepared baking dish. Top with one-third of the turkey, one-third of the soup mixture and one-third of the cheese mixture. Repeat layers twice, ending with cheese. Cover and refrigerate overnight.

When ready to cook, heat oven to 350°F (175°C). Bake casserole, covered, for 35 minutes. Remove cover; bake for 10 minutes longer, or until cheese browns.

PHEASANT DINNER PIE

4 SERVINGS

This recipe is a great way to utilize the meat left over from preparing a game stock. It's relatively easy to make and provides a delicious meal that will easily feed four hungry people.

Packaged or homemade pie crust for double-crust pie

2 tablespoons (30 g) butter

2 tablespoons (15 g) all-purpose flour

1½ cups (3.5 dl) gamebird stock (page 8) or chicken broth

½ cup (1.2 dl) heavy cream

1½ cups (210 g) cut-up cooked pheasant or other gamebird meat*

¾ cup (100 g) sliced or diced carrots, parboiled

¾ cup (115 g) diced potatoes, parboiled

½ cup (100 g) frozen peas

Rosemary, thyme, salt and pepper

Heat oven to 425°F (220°C). Fit 1 rolled-out pie crust into 9-inch (23-cm) pie plate; set aside.

In small sauté pan over low heat, make a simple roux by combining butter and flour, cooking and stirring until smooth and bubbly.

In large skillet, heat stock to boiling over high heat. When stock boils, stir in roux. Boil for about 1 minute, then reduce heat and simmer for 2 or 3 minutes (longer if possible; this helps develop flavor**). Add cream and heat to boiling. Stir in pheasant, carrots, potatoes and peas; add rosemary, thyme, salt and pepper to taste. Scrape mixture into prepared pie crust. Cover with remaining crust; seal and trim edges. Cover edge with 3-inch (7.5-cm) strips of foil (this prevents excess browning). Bake for 35 to 40 minutes, or until golden brown; remove foil for the last 15 minutes of cooking.

STOCK TIPS

You can get the meat necessary to make this meal by picking the bones of a pheasant or grouse carcass while you're making stock. Using tongs, remove the carcasses from the stockpot about an hour after the stock begins to simmer; the meat will still have plenty of flavor. The best meat is on the breastbone, around the wings, on the back and around the upper parts of the thighs. Pick what you need and return the carcass to the stockpot.

***It's best if you allow the roux-thickened stock to simmer for half an hour, skimming any skin that forms on the surface. You're making what the French call a veloute sauce, and it's delicious.*

PEKING GAMEBIRD

This recipe is great with pheasant, ruffed grouse or any light-meat upland bird. It has some real zing! Serve over a bed of white rice.

2 skinless pheasant or other upland gamebird breasts (5 to 6 ounces/142 to 170 g each), split in half, cooked*

¼ cup (60 ml) honey

¼ cup (60 ml) soy sauce

2 tablespoons (9 g) minced fresh gingerroot

2 teaspoons (10 ml) rice vinegar

¼ teaspoon (.5 g) cayenne pepper

Heat oven to 325°F (163°C). Place cooked breast halves in glass baking dish. In mixing bowl, combine remaining ingredients; pour over breast halves. Bake for 15 minutes, or until glazed (if breast halves were cooked in advance and refrigerated, you may need to bake slightly longer to warm meat completely).

***Cooking Tip**

Cook the breast halves by grilling or braising, as you prefer. They can be prepared in advance when you are cooking another meal, and refrigerated until needed; or, cook them as the first step in preparing this dish.

CREAMED WILD TURKEY

4 SERVINGS

Here's a great recipe for leftover turkey.

2 cups (4.6 dl) milk

½ cup (55 g) shredded cheddar cheese

¼ cup (12 g) snipped fresh chives

2 tablespoons (30 g) butter

1 teaspoon (6 g) garlic salt

Paprika, salt and pepper

A small amount of roux (page 118)

2 cups (280 g) cut-up cooked turkey meat

In large skillet, combine milk, cheese, chives, butter, garlic salt, and paprika, salt and pepper to taste. Heat over medium heat, stirring constantly, until boiling. Stirring constantly, add roux, a bit at a time, until sauce thickens slightly. Reduce heat so mixture simmers. Add turkey; cover and cook for 10 minutes.

ORIENTAL GROUSE SALAD

4 TO 6 SERVINGS

This is one of our favorite recipes.

1 cup (255 g) mayonnaise

¼ cup (60 ml) soy sauce

1 head Napa cabbage, cut into bite-size pieces

8 ounces (225 g) fresh mushrooms, sliced

1 cup (135 g) slivered almonds

1 can (8 ounces/227 g) sliced water chestnuts, drained

2 cups (280 g) cut-up grilled ruffed grouse breast

1 cup (45 g) chow mein noodles

In small bowl, combine mayonnaise and soy sauce, stirring to blend. In large salad bowl, combine cabbage, mushrooms, almonds and water chestnuts; toss gently. Arrange grouse pieces on top. Pour mayonnaise mixture over grouse; sprinkle with chow mein noodles.

CHAPTER FIVE

WATERFOWL
R E C I P E S

FOR MANY FORTUNATE FAMILIES, ROAST WILD GOOSE HAS BECOME TRADITIONAL HOLIDAY FARE. DEDICATED WATERFOWLERS THINK NOTHING OF SETTING OUT HOURS BEFORE DAWN, THEN WAITING IN THE COLD AND DAMP FOR A CHANCE AT A MAGNIFICENT CANADA GOOSE TO GRACE THEIR TABLE.

Wild geese and ducks are more robustly flavored than domestic waterfowl. Geese have a milder flavor than ducks, and may be a better choice for serving to those who have never tasted wild waterfowl.

Large ducks, such as mallards, canvasbacks, black ducks and redheads will generally serve two people each. Gadwalls, widgeons, wood ducks, pintails, ringnecks, scaups and goldeneyes are smaller; three ducks will serve four. Allow one teal per person.

A Canada goose will serve from three to eight people, depending on its size. Blue geese, snow geese and white-fronted geese are smaller than most Canadas, and usually serve two to six each.

The Appendix (page 120) chart on waterfowl substitutions will help you choose an alternative in case you don't have the bird called for in the recipe.

TIPS FOR PREPARING WATERFOWL

• If possible, birds to be served whole should be plucked rather than skinned. The skin helps keep the meat moist.

• To determine the degree of doneness, prick the bird with a fork. If the juices are rosy, the bird is rare. The meat will be slightly springy to the touch; internal temperature will be 145°F to 150°F (63°C to 66°C).

• Well-done birds should read 180°F (82°C); juices will run clear. The drumstick should wiggle freely in the joint.

DUCK DELIGHTS

4 TO 6 SERVINGS

Serve these delicious rolls with potatoes or wild rice.

1 tablespoon (15 g) butter

1 boneless, skinless duck breast
(6 to 8 ounces/170 to 225 g),
split in half

1½ cups (3.5 dl) duck stock
(page 8), or ¾ cup (1.8 dl)
beef broth mixed with ½ cup
(1.2 dl) chicken broth

½ teaspoon (.3 g) dried
rosemary

½ teaspoon (.4 g) dried thyme

2 bay leaves

8 ounces (225 g) cream cheese,
softened

1 can (10 ¾ ounces/305 g)
cream of mushroom soup

¼ cup (100 g) chopped carrots

2 tablespoons (30 ml) heavy
cream

1 teaspoon (3 g) minced garlic

Half of a small onion, chopped

Salt and pepper

1 tube (8 ounces/225 g)
refrigerated crescent rolls

Melted butter for brushing rolls

¾ cup (80 g) crushed croutons
or fresh breadcrumbs,
approximate

Heat oven to 250°F (120°C). In large skillet, melt butter over medium heat. Add breasts; brown on both sides. Transfer breasts to covered roaster; add stock, rosemary, thyme and bay leaves. Braise for 2 hours, or until tender. Transfer breasts to plate*; increase oven to 350°F (175°C). When duck is cool enough to handle, shred meat with your fingers.

In large mixing bowl, combine duck meat, cream cheese, soup, carrots, cream, garlic, onion, and salt and pepper to taste; mix well.

Separate crescent rolls, laying flat on work surface. Spoon duck mixture over rolls; pinch rolls together over filling to seal. Brush rolls with melted butter; roll in crushed croutons. Arrange rolls on baking sheet. Bake until golden brown, about 25 minutes.

*DUCK DELIGHT GRAVY

If you would like a gravy to serve with the Duck Delights, strain and reserve the braising liquid from the roaster. While rolls are baking, place liquid in saucepan and heat to boiling over medium heat. Stir in a small amount of roux (page 118), or cornstarch mixed in cold water or white wine. Cook, stirring constantly, until gravy reaches the desired consistency. The gravy is excellent with potatoes or wild rice, and can even be poured over the finished rolls if you like.

BRAISED CANADA GOOSE WITH ORANGE SAUCE

4 TO 8 SERVINGS, DEPENDING ON SIZE OF GOOSE

Many recipes for Canada goose produce a dry, flavorless bird. That's a shame, because Canada goose is a wonderful-tasting bird if you know how to fix it. Here's a recipe everyone in your family is sure to enjoy, especially if it is served with wild rice or mashed potatoes. This recipe is for an average-size bird. Because Canada geese vary greatly in size, you may have to make some adjustments if you're fixing a bird that weighs 10 pounds (4.5 kg) or more.

1 dressed, plucked Canada goose (5 to 7 pounds/2.3 to 3.2 kg dressed weight)

Half of an onion

3 carrots, chopped

3 ribs celery, chopped

2 cups (4.6 dl) goose stock (page 8) or enhanced chicken broth (page 8)

1½ cups (3.5 dl) dry red wine, divided

¾ cup (1.8 dl) fresh orange juice

¼ teaspoon (.5 g) dry mustard powder

Salt and pepper

A small amount of roux (page 118), or cornstarch dissolved in white wine or cold water

Heat oven to 250°F (120°C). Wash goose inside and out; pat dry with paper towels. Stuff goose cavity with onion, carrots and celery. Place stuffed goose in roasting pan; add stock and 1 cup (2.3 dl) of the wine. Cover roaster; bake for 2 hours, or until juices run clear when goose is pricked (remove cover for final 15 minutes of roasting; this makes the skin crispy and brown). De-bone cooked goose, keeping the breast in complete halves (don't slice breast meat) and the leg/thigh portions in 1 large piece per side. Set aside, covered.

Remove fat from roasting pan using bulb baster or large spoon. Strain braising liquid carefully through cheesecloth, then place in large saucepan. Add remaining ½ cup (1.2 dl) wine, the orange juice, mustard, and salt and pepper to taste. Heat over medium-high heat until boiling. Stirring constantly, add roux, a bit at a time, until sauce thickens slightly. Taste and adjust seasonings if necessary. Add goose pieces, and cook just long enough to warm through.

APPLE CINNAMON DUCK

4 SERVINGS

Whether you're in the kitchen or field, this recipe is easy to prepare and clean up. Apples help keep the duck moist, and the cinnamon adds delicious flavor to this dish.

4 bone-in whole duck breasts, skin-on or skinless (9 to 13 ounces/255 to 370 g each)

Cinnamon

2 medium-size apples, cored, peeled and sliced

Heat oven to 350°F (175°C). Line shallow baking dish with large piece of foil, allowing excess to hang over edges. Place duck breasts, bone side down, in prepared dish. Sprinkle with cinnamon to taste. Cover with apple slices; sprinkle apple slices with more cinnamon. Pour a small amount of water around edges of duck breasts; close and seal foil. Bake until meat is tender, 12 to 15 minutes.

Roast Goose Breast

3 TO 6 SERVINGS, DEPENDING ON SIZE OF GOOSE

Here's a way to "cook your goose" so it comes out tender and tasty. Serve with potatoes or wild rice.

3 slices bacon

1 boneless, skinless goose breast (about 2 pounds/900 g)

Salt and pepper

1½ cups (3.5 dl) goose stock (page 8) or chicken broth

1 cup (2.3 dl) white wine, plus additional for cornstarch mixture below

2 medium onions, sliced

3 bay leaves

Fresh or dried thyme

1 tablespoon (8 g) cornstarch, dissolved in a glass of wine

Heat oven to 300°F (150°C). In Dutch oven, fry bacon over medium heat until crisp. Transfer bacon to plate; set aside for use in another recipe.

Split goose breast in half; season with salt and pepper to taste. In bacon drippings remaining in Dutch oven, brown goose breasts very well on both sides. Add stock, wine, onions, bay leaves, and thyme to taste to Dutch oven. Cover and bake for 4 hours; check occasionally, and replace any liquid that has cooked away during roasting.

When goose breasts are tender, remove and set aside on warm platter. Pour braising liquid through sieve; discard vegetables. Return liquid to Dutch oven. Heat to boiling over medium-high heat. Stirring constantly, add cornstarch mixture; cook, stirring constantly, until liquid thickens into a gravy. Slice goose breasts and pour gravy over meat.

Gourmet Duck

4 SERVINGS

This quick, easy recipe is a foolproof way to make moist, flavorful duck.

1½ cups (120 g) chopped mushrooms

½ cup (65 g) chopped carrot

2 ribs celery, chopped

½ cup (110 g/1 stick) butter, divided

1 jar (8 ounces/225 g) currant jelly

1½ cups (3.5 dl) bourbon

2 tablespoons (30 ml) dry sherry

Salt and pepper

2 boneless, skinless duck breasts (6 to 8 ounces/170 to 225 g each), split in half

In large skillet, sauté mushrooms, carrot and celery in ¼ cup (55 g/half of a stick) of the butter over medium heat until vegetables are tender; set aside.

In saucepan, melt remaining ¼ cup (55 g/half of a stick) butter over medium heat. Add jelly; cook, stirring frequently, until jelly melts. Add bourbon, sherry, and salt and pepper to taste. Heat to boiling.

Pour jelly mixture into skillet with vegetables. Heat to boiling over medium heat. Add duck breasts. Cook for 15 minutes, then turn and continue cooking for 10 minutes longer.

EASY WATERFOWL APPETIZER

8 TO 10 APPETIZER SERVINGS

Make a wonderful hors d'oeuvre from goose or duck breast with this easy recipe.

2 boneless, skinless duck breasts (6 to 8 ounces/170 to 225 g each); or 1 goose breast

2 cans (8 ounces/227 g each) whole water chestnuts, drained

1 pound (454 g) sliced bacon

1 cup (2.3 dl) soy sauce

1 bottle (12 ounces/3.5 dl) teriyaki sauce

Sweet and sour dipping sauce, hot mustard, or other dipping sauce(s) of your choice

Slice breast halves into thin strips. Place whole water chestnut on middle of a strip; wrap with bacon and secure with wooden tooth-pick. In mixing bowl, combine soy sauce and teriyaki sauce. Add bacon-wrapped bundles; cover and refrigerate for about 2 hours.

When ready to cook, heat oven to 325°F (163°C). Drain bacon-wrapped bundles; arrange on baking sheet. Bake for 40 minutes, or until bacon is golden brown. Serve hot, with dipping sauce(s).

ELAINE'S DUCK

4 SERVINGS

This is a great recipe for tasty and juicy ducks. Serve over noodles; fresh broccoli is a good complement to this dish.

1/2 cup (70 g) all-purpose flour

1 tablespoon (18 g) seasoning salt

1/4 teaspoon (.5 g) black pepper

2 boneless, skinless duck breasts (6 to 8 ounces/170 to 225 g each), split in half

2 tablespoons (30 ml) vegetable oil

1/4 cup (40 g) chopped onion

1 tablespoon (15 g) butter

2 cans (10 3/4 ounces/305 g each) cream of mushroom soup

1/3 cup (80 ml) milk

1/4 cup (60 ml) white cooking wine, optional

In clean paper bag, shake together flour, seasoning salt and pepper. Add breasts; shake to coat. In medium skillet, fry breasts in oil over medium-high heat until golden brown on both sides. Transfer breasts to paper towels to drain.

In medium saucepan, sauté onion in butter over medium heat until transparent. Add soup, milk and wine. Adjust heat so mixture simmers; cook for 10 minutes. Add duck pieces; simmer for 10 to 15 minutes longer.

MARINATED DUCK BREAST WITH BACON HORS D'OEUVRES

6 TO 8 APPETIZER SERVINGS

This is a simple yet delicious duck recipe.

2 boneless, skinless duck breasts (6 to 8 ounces/170 to 225 g each), split in half

1 cup (2.3 dl) milk

1/2 cup (1.2 dl) red wine

1/4 cup (60 ml) vegetable oil

1/4 cup (60 ml) soy sauce

1 teaspoon (3 g) crushed garlic

4 slices bacon

1 tablespoon (15 ml) rhubarb jam*

1 tablespoon (15 ml) strawberry jam*

1 teaspoon (5 ml) white vinegar

In mixing bowl, marinate breasts in milk overnight. The next day, drain and pat dry. Rinse out mixing bowl; combine wine, oil, soy sauce and garlic in bowl. Add breasts; cover and refrigerate for 3 hours.

When ready to cook, prepare charcoal or gas grill. Drain duck breast halves; pat dry. Wrap each breast half with bacon slice. Grill for about 7 minutes on each side, or until desired doneness.

While duck is grilling, prepare sauce: In small saucepan, combine rhubarb and strawberry jams with vinegar. Heat over low heat, stirring constantly, until jam melts and mixture is warm and well combined. Serve sauce with duck.

> ***JAM NOTE**
> *You may substitute 2 tablespoons (30 ml) of strawberry-rhubarb jam if you can' t find the individual flavors at your store.*

PRESSURED GOOSE

4 TO 8 SERVINGS, DEPENDING ON SIZE OF GOOSE

1 dressed, plucked goose (about 8 pounds/3.6 kg)

1 can (14 ounces/4.2 dl) roasted garlic chicken broth

1 1/2 teaspoons (3 g) Cajun seasoning blend (purchased, or prepared from the recipe on page 13)

2 tablespoons plus 1 1/2 teaspoons (45 g) garlic salt

Put goose in 8-quart (7.6 l) pressure cooker. Pour remaining ingredients over the top, in the order listed. Seal cooker, and cook according to the pressure-cooker manufacturer's instructions. If you don't have instructions, here's how I do it. Set pressure for 10 pounds. Heat over high heat until the pressure control jiggles, then adjust heat so control jiggles 3 times per minute. Start timing and cook for 20 to 25 minutes.

Remove pressure cooker from heat and let stand for 10 minutes at room temperature, then run the cooker under cold water until you can open it (or, follow manufacturer's directions for quickly reducing pressure). Place goose on platter; make gravy if desired from juices remaining in cooker.

CHAPTER SIX

STARTERS & SIDE DISHES

MANY OF THE RECIPES THROUGHOUT THIS BOOK COULD BE PREPARED AS AN APPETIZER TO GET YOUR MEAL GOING. REMEMBER TO SERVE SMALL HELPINGS OF APPETIZERS TO STIMULATE THE APPETITE BUT NOT SATISFY IT.

A meal starter definitely sets the scene for the rest of the meal and, often, the occasion.

Some dishes just naturally go with fish or wild game. Their ingredients are also natural or wild. The experience of hunting for morels and other edible mushrooms, for instance, can add to the dish by providing memories of a trip in the outdoors.

Many dishes, especially starters and side dishes like vegetables and salads, not only taste good but also add color and appeal to the meal.

TIPS FOR PREPARING STARTERS & SIDE DISHES

• Soups can be light and delicate, or rich and hearty—to warm you in the winter or as a refreshing treat on a hot summer day.

• Of course, many ingredients can be purchased in a local store, but what fun to buy them from a vendor who freshly harvested them.

Crunchy Mashed Sweet Potatoes

This delightful dish takes longer to prepare than many other sweet potato recipes, but it's worth the effort.

Butter for greasing dish

5 large sweet potatoes, peeled and cut into 2-inch (5-cm) pieces

3 large eggs

2 tablespoons (30 ml) maple syrup

2 tablespoons (30 ml) vanilla extract

3/4 cup (165 g) packed brown sugar

1/4 cup (55 g/half of a stick) chilled butter, cut into small pieces

1 1/2 cups (135 g) crushed cornflakes

Heat oven to 350°F (175°C). Lightly butter glass casserole dish. Heat large pot of salted water to boiling over high heat. Add sweet potatoes; boil until tender, about 15 minutes. Drain well; mash with potato masher.

In large mixing bowl, combine eggs, syrup and vanilla; beat with fork. Add mashed potatoes; blend thoroughly. Transfer mixture to prepared baking dish. In mixing bowl, blend together brown sugar and butter until coarse. Sprinkle over potato mixture; top with crushed cornflakes. Bake for 1 hour; remove from oven and let stand for 10 minutes before serving.

Mashed Potatoes and Sweet Potatoes

6 SERVINGS

Few side dishes I've served get the compliments this one does. It goes great with barbecue dishes.

Butter for greasing dish

6 large cloves garlic, peeled and cut in half

A few drops of olive oil

2 pounds (900 g) potatoes, peeled and cut into chunks

2 pounds (900 g) sweet potatoes, peeled and cut into chunks

1/2 teaspoon (.3 g) dried rosemary leaves

1/4 cup (55 g/half of a stick) butter

Salt and pepper

Heavy cream, as needed

Heat oven to 350°F (175°C). Lightly butter glass casserole dish; set aside. Place garlic cloves on small piece of foil; drizzle with oil. Wrap foil around garlic. Bake until soft, about 20 minutes.

Meanwhile, heat large pot of salted water to boiling over high heat. Add potatoes, sweet potatoes and rosemary; boil until tender, about 20 minutes. Drain well; return to pot. Add roasted garlic, butter, and salt and pepper to taste; mash with potato masher, adding cream as needed for desired texture.

Transfer to prepared casserole dish; cover and allow to sit at room temperature for 1 or 2 hours (this allows the flavors to infuse). Re-heat oven if necessary to 350°F (175°C). Uncover casserole; bake for 30 minutes, or until top begins to brown.

Garlic-Herb Mashed Potatoes

4 SERVINGS

Over the years I've seen dozens of recipes for garlic- and herb-flavored mashed potatoes. I've always wanted to try them, but the fresh herbs required haven't been available at the local supermarket. I was lamenting this problem to a friend and she suggested using a soft cheese with garlic and herbs incorporated, like Boursin. This very simple recipe was the result. These potatoes are quick and delicious, and go well with a variety of dishes.

1 pound (454 g) potatoes, peeled and cut into chunks

¼ cup (60 g) soft garlic-and-herb cheese such as Boursin

Salt and pepper

Dried parsley flakes

Buttermilk, as needed

Heat large pot of salted water to boiling over high heat. Add potatoes; boil until tender, about 15 minutes. Drain well; return to pot.

Add cheese, and salt, pepper and parsley to taste; mash with potato masher, adding buttermilk a little at a time until potatoes are desired texture.

Wild Rice and Mushrooms

4 TO 6 SERVINGS

Nothing goes with game and fish like wild rice and mushrooms. This particular version can be used as a stuffing, or can be baked in the oven as a side dish.

Butter for greasing dish

2 tablespoons (30 g) butter, preferably unsalted

1 cup (95 g) finely chopped mushrooms

½ cup (100 g) finely chopped onion

¼ cup (40 g) finely chopped celery

1 tablespoon (15 g) minced garlic

2 cups (300 g) cooked wild rice

¼ cup (15 g) chopped fresh parsley

½ teaspoon (.4 g) dried thyme

½ teaspoon (.2 g) dried rubbed sage

Salt and pepper

Heat oven to 350°F (175°C). Butter glass baking dish; set aside. In medium skillet, melt butter over medium heat. Add mushrooms, onion, celery and garlic. Cook, stirring occasionally, until vegetables are soft. Add rice, parsley, thyme, sage, and salt and pepper to taste; mix well. Transfer to prepared baking dish. Cover and bake for 20 minutes, or until heated through.

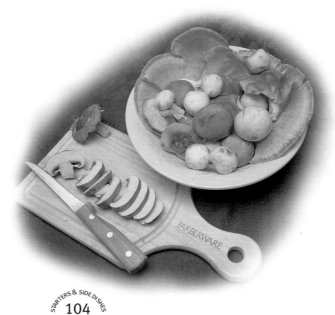

CREAM OF MOREL SOUP

4 TO 6 SERVINGS

While this recipe is wonderful with morel mushrooms, it would work with any wild mushroom. It's a great appetizer for any wild game dinner.

- ¼ cup (55 g/half of a stick) butter
- 1 pound (454 g) morel mushrooms, sliced
- ½ cup (1.2 dl) dry white wine
- 1 quart (.95 l) pheasant stock (page 8) or chicken broth
- ½ cup (1.2 dl) heavy cream
- Dried thyme
- Salt and pepper

In large saucepan, melt butter over medium heat. When butter stops foaming, add mushrooms. Cook, stirring occasionally, until juices given up by mushrooms have reduced to a few tablespoons (about 30 ml). (If you like, reserve a few cooked mushrooms for garnishing the soup later.) Add wine; boil for a few minutes. Add stock; reduce heat and simmer for about 5 minutes. Remove from heat and allow to cool slightly, then carefully pour into blender or food processor and purée until smooth.

Return puréed soup to saucepan. Add cream, and thyme, salt and pepper to taste. Heat briefly before serving; garnish with cooked, reserved mushrooms if you like.

CABBAGE-AND-GARLIC MASHED POTATOES

4 TO 6 SERVINGS

You may be thinking that this doesn't sound very appetizing. Think again. It's one of the most delicious potato dishes I've ever tried!

- 2 pounds (454 g) potatoes, cubed
- 2 large cloves garlic, chopped
- 2 tablespoons (30 g) butter
- One-quarter of a head of white cabbage, finely shredded
- Salt and pepper
- Chopped fresh parsley
- Buttermilk, as needed

Heat large pot of salted water to boiling over high heat. Add potatoes; cook until tender, 10 to 15 minutes. Remove from heat and set aside.

In large skillet, sauté garlic in butter until lightly browned. Add cabbage; cook until slightly softened, stirring frequently. Meanwhile, drain potatoes. Add cabbage mixture and salt, pepper and parsley to taste. Mash potatoes, adding enough buttermilk to make potatoes fluffy.

PLAIN WILD RICE

ABOUT 2 CUPS (300 G) COOKED WILD RICE

Here's a basic recipe for cooking wild rice to use in other dishes, or to serve on its own as a side dish. If you like, you can add sautéed slivered almonds or mushrooms just before serving.

1 cup (180 g) uncooked wild rice

1½ cups (3.5 dl) chicken broth or water

In saucepan, combine wild rice and broth. Cover and place over medium-low heat. Adjust heat so liquid simmers; cook until rice "pops" or opens up, usually about 30 minutes (but this may vary, depending on the type of wild rice you are cooking).

WILD RICE SOUP

4 TO 6 SERVINGS

This recipe takes almost no time to prepare and it's a wonderful starter for any wild game meal.

1 onion, diced

2 tablespoons (30 ml) canola oil or butter

10 ounces (280 g) fresh mushrooms, sliced or cut up as you prefer

2 cups (300 g) cooked wild rice

½ pound (225 g) sliced bacon, browned and crumbled

1 pound (454 g) Velveeta cheese, cubed

1 quart (.95 l) half-and-half

In large saucepan, sauté onion in oil over medium heat until tender. Add mushrooms; continue cooking until mushrooms are tender. Add remaining ingredients; cook until cheese melts, stirring frequently.

WILD RICE SOUFFLÉ

4 SERVINGS

I honestly don't know where I got this recipe. Someone sent it to the office, but the return address was lost and the sender didn't sign his or her name. Despite the fact that "wild rice soufflé" sounds like an oxymoron, we tried it and it was wonderful. Give it a try and I think you'll agree.

Butter for greasing pan

1 small onion, finely diced

A pinch each of dried rosemary and thyme

¼ cup (55 g/half of a stick) butter

1 cup (140 g) all-purpose flour

2 cups (300 g) cooked wild rice

2 cups (4.6 dl) heavy cream

4 egg whites

Heat oven to 375°F (190°C). Butter standard-size loaf pan; set aside.

In large nonstick skillet, sauté onion, rosemary and thyme in butter over medium heat until onion is soft. Reduce heat slightly and add flour, stirring constantly to prevent lumps. Add wild rice and cream; stir well and remove from heat to cool slightly.

Meanwhile, in large mixing bowl, beat egg whites with electric mixer until stiff peaks form. Add cooled rice mixture to egg whites, folding in quickly but gently. Scrape mixture into prepared pan. Bake for 1½ hours, or until soufflé starts to brown on top.

MORELS AND STUFFING

6 SERVINGS

This recipe goes particularly well with fried fish. Since the opening of fishing season coincides with the emergence of morel mushrooms, that makes it a great combination. If you're not a morel-picker, any of the wild mushrooms now available in most grocery stores will work. If wild mushrooms aren't available, button mushrooms will do.

3 tablespoons (45 g) butter, divided, plus additional for greasing dish

3/4 cup (150 g) finely diced onion

1 cup (120 g) finely diced celery

2 cloves garlic, minced

5 cups (200 g) croutons

1 egg, lightly beaten

1 1/4 cups (2.9 dl) pheasant stock (page 8) or chicken broth, divided

Dried rubbed sage, rosemary and thyme

3 cups (210 g) sliced morels* or other mushrooms

3 tablespoons (45 ml) heavy cream

2 tablespoons (30 ml) white wine

Salt and pepper

A small amount of roux (page 118)

Heat oven to 375°F (190°C). Butter 2-quart (1.9 l) casserole dish; set aside. In sauté pan, cook onion, celery and garlic in 2 tablespoons (30 g) of the butter over medium heat until tender.

Transfer to large mixing bowl. Add croutons, egg, 1 cup (2.3 dl) stock, and sage, rosemary and thyme to taste (don't be afraid to use plenty of herbs); mix until croutons have absorbed all the stock. Transfer mixture to prepared casserole dish. Bake for 1 hour, or until stuffing is cooked through and becoming crispy on top.

Meanwhile, prepare the sauce: In same sauté pan, cook morels in remaining 1 tablespoon (15 g) butter until they give up their liquid. Add cream, wine, remaining 1/4 cup (60 ml) stock, and rosemary, thyme, salt and pepper to taste. Cook until reduced by half. Stirring constantly, add roux, a bit at a time, until sauce thickens slightly. To serve, spoon stuffing onto plates; top with mushroom sauce.

*MUSHROOM PREPARATION

Here's a tip for washing morels or any mushroom. Always rinse the mushrooms in cold water and place them on paper towels. Do not soak the mushrooms in water. Morels are wet mushrooms and should be kept as dry as possible.

"Squashed" Potatoes

We had this side dish in a restaurant once and liked it so much we started experimenting with ways to prepare it at home. It's a very simple recipe that goes well with any wild game but is especially good with venison and duck. Preparation time is just minutes, but it's sure to bring rave reviews from your guests. This dish can be prepared ahead of time and reheated in an uncovered casserole at 350°F (175°C) for 30 minutes.

1 butternut squash

5 cloves garlic, peeled and halved

Potatoes to equal weight of squash

½ cup (110 g/1 stick) butter

Salt and pepper

Heat oven to 350°F (175°C). Cut squash in half lengthwise; remove and discard seeds. Place in glass baking dish, cut side down. Add water to come 1 inch (2.5 cm) up the sides of dish. Scatter garlic halves around squash. Bake until tender, 25 to 40 minutes depending on size of squash. Meanwhile, peel and slice potatoes. Cook in large pot of boiling, salted water until tender. When squash is tender, scoop flesh from shell; discard shell. Drain potatoes. Mash together squash, potatoes and garlic, adding butter as you mash. Season to taste with salt and pepper. Top each serving with a pat of butter.

Creamy Mushroom Soup

4 TO 6 SERVINGS

Have you ever eaten a truly sumptuous cream of mushroom soup at a fine restaurant? This is that kind of soup. Its rich flavor makes it a perfect starter for any wild game meal.

1 pound (454 g) fresh button mushrooms

¼ cup (55 g/half of a stick) butter, divided

2 tablespoons (30 ml) canola oil

1 cup (160 g) finely chopped shallots

3 tablespoons (22 g) all-purpose flour

3 cups (6.9 dl) gamebird stock (page 8) or chicken broth

3 cups (6.9 dl) half-and-half

¼ cup plus 1 tablespoon (75 ml) heavy cream

Fresh chopped basil or dried basil

Salt and pepper

Remove stems from mushrooms. Slice caps thinly; chop stems. In large saucepan, melt 2 tablespoons (27.5 g) of the butter in the oil over medium heat. Add shallots, the chopped mushroom stems and about two-thirds of the sliced mushroom caps. Cook until mushrooms are soft, stirring occasionally. Reduce heat; cover and cook for about 5 minutes longer. Remove cover; add flour, stirring constantly to prevent lumps. Add stock and half-and-half. Increase heat to medium-high. Heat to boiling, then reduce heat and simmer for 10 minutes, stirring occasionally. Remove from heat; set aside to cool slightly.

While soup is cooling, sauté remaining sliced mushroom caps in remaining 2 tablespoons (27.5 g) butter. When soup has cooled slightly, carefully pour into blender or food processor and purée until smooth. Return puréed soup to saucepan. Add sautéed mushrooms, cream, and basil, salt and pepper to taste.

WILD RICE AND MUSHROOM RISOTTO

4 SERVINGS

This is the perfect accompaniment for just about any wild game dish. It really isn't that difficult or complicated to prepare, although it does dirty a lot of pots and pans. But I think you'll agree, it's worth it.

6 cups (1.4 l) game stock (page 8) or chicken broth, divided

1 cup (180 g) uncooked wild rice

2 tablespoons (30 ml) extra-virgin olive oil

1 medium onion, minced

1 cup (190 g) Arborio rice

½ cup (1.2 dl) dry white wine

2 tablespoons (30 g) butter, divided

1 cup (70 g) sliced fresh mushrooms

Half of a red bell pepper, seeded and diced

½ cup (63 g) freshly grated Parmesan cheese

Salt and freshly ground black pepper

RISOTTO COOKING TIPS

• *Never cover risotto during preparation.*

• *It's amazing how much stock the rice can absorb. Add the final cup (2.3 dl) of stock a bit at a time. You don't want the rice to become mushy.*

• *If available, get fresh Parmesan and grate it yourself.*

In medium saucepan, combine 2 cups (4.6 dl) of the stock with the wild rice. Cover and cook over low heat until the rice is almost tender. While wild rice is cooking, place remaining 4 cups (.95 l) of the stock in another medium saucepan. Heat over medium heat until simmering; adjust heat and allow to simmer during rice preparation.

While wild rice continues to cook, heat oil in large, heavy nonstick skillet over medium heat. Add onion; cook until soft but not brown. Increase heat slightly; add Arborio rice, stirring to coat rice with oil. Cook, stirring frequently, for about 3 minutes; rice will begin to look chalky. Stir in wine, and continue cooking until wine has been absorbed. Add 1 cup (2.3 dl) of the simmering stock; continue cooking, stirring frequently, until stock has been absorbed. Add another cup (2.3 dl) of stock; continue cooking, stirring frequently, until stock has been absorbed.

While rice is cooking, melt 1 tablespoon (15 g) of the butter in medium skillet over medium heat. Add mushrooms and bell pepper; sauté until vegetables are browned and tender. By now, the wild rice should be cooked, and the Arborio rice should have absorbed the second cup (2.3 dl) of stock. Measure out 1 cup (150 g) of the cooked wild rice; add to Arborio rice (reserve any remaining cooked wild rice for another use). Add another cup (2.3 dl) of simmering stock to the Arborio rice, along with sautéed vegetables. Cook, stirring frequently, until stock has been absorbed.

At this point, begin tasting the Arborio rice. The grains should be tender, but firm in the center rather than mushy. If it's too firm, stir in additional stock, ½ cup (1.2 dl) at a time, cooking after each addition, until tender-firm. Remove rice from heat; stir in remaining 1 tablespoon (15 g) of butter, the Parmesan cheese, and salt and pepper to taste. Let stand for a few minutes before serving.

CHAPTER SEVEN

SAUCES & MARINADES

SAUCES CAN ENHANCE THE FLAVOR OF SIMPLY PREPARED FISH AND GAME. MARINADES TENDERIZE TOUGHER CUTS OF GAME AND ADD FLAVOR.

Game stock is ideal for use in the sauce recipes that call for stock. A good sauce should not cover the natural flavor of the fish or game. It can be simple or complex, but I find that it always adds a unique flavor.

Most marinades are a combination of oil and an acidic element such as vinegar, lemon juice or wine, with herbs and spices added for flavor. You can experiment with different ingredients and seasoning combinations to create your own "house blend."

TIPS FOR PREPARING SAUCES & MARINADES

• If you use prepared chicken or beef broth instead of homemade stock, you may want to reduce the amount of salt in the recipe.

• For extra tang, substitute fish stock for the water, the wine, or half of the milk or cream in the sauce recipe.

• The oil in a marinade can add moisture to meat that has little natural fat, such as venison.

• If you like lots of sauce, just double the recipe!

LEMON-BUTTER SAUCE

ABOUT 3/4 CUP (1.8 DL)

One of our favorite restaurants features an appetizer of crab cakes with lemon-butter sauce. With a glass of white wine, it's so delicious we sometimes go there just to have this appetizer, skipping the main course. The chef refused to share his secret with us, so we experimented until we came up with a version just as good. When making the sauce, be sure to stir the butter in, one pat at a time, over low heat; if you rush the butter, all you'll wind up with is flavored melted butter.

Half to three-quarters of a fresh lemon, sliced

1 shallot, diced

¼ cup (60 ml) champagne vinegar

1 cup (2.3 dl) white wine*

1 tablespoon (4 g) coarsely chopped fresh parsley*

1 teaspoon (.75 g) dried thyme*

½ cup (1.2 dl) heavy cream

¾ cup (165 g/1 ½ sticks) cold, unsalted butter, cut into small pieces

Fresh or dried dill weed

Salt and pepper

In small enamel or stainless-steel saucepan, combine lemon slices, shallot and vinegar. Heat to boiling over medium heat. Add wine, parsley and thyme. Increase heat to medium-high; cook until reduced by half. Add cream; continue cooking until reduced by half. Remove from heat. Add butter, a pat at a time, stirring after each addition until all butter has been melted in and sauce is smooth and silky (if pan gets too cool, place over edge of burner on lowest heat for a few seconds, then remove from heat and continue). Strain sauce, discarding solids. Season to taste with dill, salt and pepper.

***RECIPE VARIATION**

For a variation to this main recipe, eliminate the wine, parsley and thyme. After vinegar has reduced, add cream and proceed as directed. Yield will be slightly less.

LEMON-DILL SAUCE

ABOUT 3/4 CUP (1.8 DL)

¼ cup plus 2 tablespoons (90 ml) white white

2 tablespoons (30 ml) white wine vinegar

3 tablespoons (30 g) chopped shallots

1 tablespoon (15 ml) heavy cream

1 tablespoon (6 g) grated lemon zest

Dried or fresh dill weed, salt and pepper

½ cup (110 g/1 stick) cold, unsalted butter, cut into small pieces

In small enamel or stainless-steel saucepan, combine wine, vinegar and shallots. Cook over medium-high heat until reduced by three-quarters. Add cream, lemon zest, and dill, salt and pepper to taste. Remove from heat. Add butter, a pat at a time, stirring after each addition until all butter has been melted in and sauce is smooth and silky.

PINEAPPLE-BASIL SAUCE

ABOUT 1¼ CUPS (2.9 DL)

This sauce goes great with just about any fish dish, but it's particularly good with baked, poached or broiled fish. Place the fish next to a bed of wild rice and drizzle the sauce over both the rice and the fish, then sit back and wait for the "ooohs" and "aaahs" from your guests. The sauce can be prepared ahead of time and stored in a covered dish in the refrigerator for several days; in fact, the flavors will incorporate nicely if you do this. Heat sauce in the microwave when it's time to serve.

½ cup (30 g) crushed fresh pineapple, or drained canned crushed pineapple

¼ cup (60 ml) white wine

¾ cup (1.8 dl) heavy cream

1 tablespoon (15 ml) freshly squeezed lemon juice

¼ teaspoon (.1 g) dried basil; or 3 leaves fresh basil, chopped

2 tablespoons (30 g) unsalted butter, cut into small pieces

Salt and pepper

Place pineapple in small enamel or stainless-steel saucepan. Heat over medium heat, shaking pan until pineapple releases its juices. Add wine; cook until reduced by half. Stir in cream; heat to boiling, stirring vigorously. Remove from heat.

Add lemon juice and basil; add butter, a pat at a time, stirring after each addition until all butter has been melted in and sauce is smooth and silky.

Place over medium heat again, and return to boiling. Add salt and pepper to taste.

MUSHROOM-CREAM SAUCE

ABOUT 1½ CUPS (3.5 DL)

After you have browned some steaks or chops, use the same skillet to prepare this sauce. The browned bits remaining in the skillet will add richness and flavor to the sauce.

8 ounces (225 g) fresh mushrooms, sliced

1 small shallot, chopped

Pan drippings from browning meat (see above), or 1 tablespoon (15 ml) vegetable oil

1 cup (2.3 dl) dry white wine

½ cup (1.2 dl) gamebird stock (page 8) or chicken broth

½ cup (1.2 dl) heavy cream

A small amount of roux (page 118)

2 tablespoons (30 g) butter

Salt and pepper

In skillet, sauté mushrooms and shallot over medium heat in drippings or oil. Cook until nicely browned, stirring occasionally. Deglaze pan by adding wine, stirring to loosen browned bits. Increase heat slightly; cook until wine has almost cooked away. Add stock and cream. Cook for a few minutes longer to reduce slightly. Stirring constantly, add roux, a bit at a time, until sauce thickens slightly. Remove from heat; stir in butter, and salt and pepper to taste.

MUSTARD BUTTER SAUCE

ABOUT 3/4 CUP (1.8 DL)

This sauce is a bit time-consuming, but it's worth the effort. It's actually a variation of beurre blanc, a French white butter sauce. The trick to making this sauce is incorporating the butter a bit at a time, whisking it constantly. When one pat is nearly melted, add another and stir vigorously until the next is nearly dissolved. Be sure to remove the pan from the heat when stirring in the butter, or the sauce will separate. An enamel saucepan seems to work best for this recipe. You can strain the sauce before serving or, if you prefer, leave the shallots in the sauce.

1/4 cup plus 2 tablespoons (90 ml) dry white wine

2 tablespoons (30 ml) white wine vinegar

3 tablespoons (30 g) minced shallots

1 tablespoon plus 1 1/2 teaspoons (22.5 ml) heavy cream

1/2 cup (110 g/1 stick) cold, unsalted butter, cut into small pieces

1 teaspoon (15 ml) lemon juice

1/2 teaspoon (2.5 g) Dijon mustard

1/2 teaspoon (2.5 g) French whole-grain mustard

In enamel or thick-walled saucepan, combine wine, vinegar and shallots. Cook over medium heat until reduced by three-quarters. Add cream; remove from heat. Add butter, a pat at a time, stirring after each addition until all butter has been melted in and sauce is smooth and silky (if pan gets too cool, place over edge of burner on lowest heat for a few seconds, then remove from heat and continue). Just before serving, stir in lemon juice, Dijon and whole-grain mustards; serve immediately.

BARBECUE SAUCE

ABOUT 2 1/2 CUPS (5.8 DL)

2 cloves garlic, minced

1/4 cup (55 g/half of a stick) butter

2 cups (4.6 dl) catsup

1/2 cup (1.2 dl) water

1/4 cup plus 2 tablespoons (80 g) packed brown sugar

2 tablespoons (30 ml) Worcestershire sauce

1 teaspoon (5 ml) liquid smoke

1/2 teaspoon (1 g) freshly ground pepper

In small saucepan, sauté garlic in butter over medium heat until soft. Add remaining ingredients; heat to boiling. Reduce heat; simmer for 5 minutes, stirring occasionally.

Mushroom-Port Sauce

ABOUT 1 CUP (2.3 DL)

This recipe got rave reviews from everyone who tried it. It's great served over gamebird pieces.

6 ounces (170 g) mushrooms, sliced

2 tablespoons (20 g) finely diced shallot

1 tablespoon (15 g) butter

¼ cup (60 ml) port wine

¼ cup (60 ml) gamebird stock (page 8) or chicken broth

1 cup (2.3 dl) heavy cream

A squirt of lemon juice

1½ teaspoons (.5 g) dried parsley flakes

Salt and pepper

In sauté pan, cook mushrooms and shallot in butter over medium heat until tender. Add port and stock, stirring to loosen any browned bits. Increase heat to medium-high; cook until mixture becomes thick and sticky. Add cream; boil until sauce begins to thicken. Remove from heat; add lemon juice, parsley, and salt and pepper to taste.

Plum Dandy Port Sauce

ABOUT 2 CUPS (4.6 DL)

This wonderful sauce works well with any dark-meat game. It can be poured over duck, goose or venison. Best of all, it's relatively easy to prepare.

2 cups (4.6 dl) port wine

½ cup (1.2 dl) orange juice

1 tablespoon (15 ml) lemon juice

1½ cups (3.5 dl) venison stock (page 9) or beef broth

1 tablespoon (15 ml) Oriental plum sauce

½ teaspoon (2.5 ml) Worcestershire sauce

1 shallot, diced

1 clove garlic, crushed

¼ cup (55 g/half of a stick) cold butter, cut into pieces

Dried parsley flakes, salt and pepper

In medium enamel or stainless-steel saucepan, heat wine to simmering over medium heat. Add orange juice and lemon juice; cook for 15 minutes longer. Add stock, plum sauce, Worcestershire sauce, shallot and garlic; cook until reduced by half. Strain, discarding solids.

Return liquid to saucepan; continue cooking until sauce thickens. Remove from heat. Add butter, a pat at a time, stirring after each addition until all butter has been melted in and sauce is smooth and silky. Season to taste with parsley, salt and pepper.

SWEET, SIMPLE ORANGE SAUCES

Nothing enhances the flavor of duck or goose like orange sauce. Take a juicy bird—preferably braised—and brown the skin until it's crispy. Then pour a rich orange sauce over the top and you've got a wonderful meal. (Use an enameled or stainless-steel saucepan.)

SAUCE #1 (ABOUT ⅓ CUP/80 ML):

½ cup (1.2 dl) frozen orange juice concentrate, thawed

¼ cup (60 ml) duck stock (page 8) or chicken broth

2 tablespoons (30 ml) Grand Marnier

1 tablespoon (15 ml) soy sauce

1 tablespoon (5 g) minced fresh gingerroot

2 tablespoons (25 g) packed brown sugar

2 tablespoons (40 g) currant jelly

2 tablespoons (30 g) butter

Salt and pepper

In medium saucepan, combine orange juice concentrate, stock, Grand Marnier, soy sauce and gingerroot. Cook over medium heat until mixture becomes syrupy. Add brown sugar and jelly; cook, stirring constantly, until jelly melts. Remove from heat; add butter, and salt and pepper to taste.

SAUCE #2 (ABOUT ¾ CUP/1.8 DL):

1 cup (2.3 dl) freshly squeezed orange juice

2 tablespoons (30 ml) balsamic vinegar

1 tablespoon (5 g) grated fresh gingerroot

1 cup (2.3 dl) duck stock (page 8) or chicken broth

3 tablespoons (45 ml) Grand Marnier

Salt and pepper

In medium saucepan, combine orange juice, vinegar and gingerroot. Cook over medium heat until reduced by half. Add stock; continue cooking until reduced by half again. Add Grand Marnier, and salt and pepper to taste.

SAUCE #3 (ABOUT ½ CUP/1.2 DL):

½ cup (1.2 dl) freshly squeezed orange juice

1 cup (2.3 dl) duck stock (page 8) or chicken broth

2 tablespoons (30 ml) Grand Marnier

2 tablespoons (30 g) butter

In medium saucepan, cook orange juice over medium heat until reduced by half. Add stock; cook until reduced by half again. Stir in Grand Marnier and butter.

SAUCE #4 (ABOUT ¾ CUP/1.8 DL):

½ cup (170 g) orange marmalade

3 tablespoons (45 ml) Grand Marnier

2 tablespoons (30 ml) soy sauce

2 tablespoons (40 g) currant jelly

1 tablespoon (5 g) grated fresh gingerroot

In medium saucepan, combine all ingredients; cook over medium heat, stirring constantly, until mixture becomes syrupy. This last recipe is a bit sweet for my taste, but some readers may find it to their liking.

Ocean Fish Marinade

ABOUT ²/₃ CUP (1.6 ML)

We like to use this marinade with shark fillets, but it works well for a wide variety of ocean fish. It makes enough for about 2 pounds (900 g) of fish fillets or steaks.

½ cup (1.2 dl) teriyaki sauce

2 tablespoons (30 ml) dry sherry

1 teaspoon (1.7 g) minced fresh gingerroot

1 clove garlic, minced

Combine all ingredients in sliding zipper-style plastic food-storage bag. Add fish fillets; flip over to marinate both sides. Refrigerate until ready to grill or broil fish.

Minnesota Marinade

ABOUT 1 3/4 CUPS (4.1 DL)

Apparently this recipe for a venison marinade has been bouncing around Minnesota longer than some of our favorite Ole and Lena jokes. We received it from several different sources. Official credit goes to Curt Johnson of the Minnesota Department of Tourism, who says he got it from Todd McDonald of the Minnesota News Network as supplied to him by Minneapolis Star Tribune outdoor writer Ron Schara. See what I mean? And that's only one of several contributors who submitted it. Anyway, here's the recipe.

½ cup (1.2 dl) cooking oil

½ cup (1.2 dl) red or white wine

½ cup (1.2 dl) catsup

2 tablespoons (30 ml) soy sauce

1 teaspoon (5 ml) Worcestershire sauce

1 teaspoon (15 ml) lemon juice

¼ teaspoon (.8 g) dry mustard powder

3 small cloves garlic, minced

In large mixing bowl, combine all ingredients, stirring to blend. Pour over venison and let stand 3 hours at room temperature. Cook meat on grill.

Kris' Marinade

1/2 CUP MARINADE (1.2 DL)

½ cup (1.2 dl) vinegar

2 teaspoons (12 g) salt

2 cloves garlic

Combine all ingredients in glass or ceramic bowl. Pour over meat and refrigerate, covered, overnight.

Bob Mitchell's Venison Marinade

ABOUT 5 1/4 CUPS (1.2 L)

Bob Mitchell is a long-time friend of our company. Bob works for Campbell Ewald, the Detroit-based advertising agency that handles Chevy Trucks. He's an avid fisherman who has joined us on a number of Canadian outings, an avid duck hunter who spends lots of time on Lake St. Clair and—based on the recipe he sent along—likes to hunt deer as well.

3 cups (6.9 dl) vegetable oil

1 cup (2.3 dl) soy sauce

1 cup (2.3 dl) honey

1/2 cup (1.2 dl) vinegar

1/2 cup (50 g) chopped green onions (white and green parts)

2 tablespoons (10 g) ground ginger

4 cloves garlic, chopped

In large mixing bowl, combine all ingredients, stirring to blend. Pour marinade over venison steaks; cover and refrigerate for 8 hours. Grill to medium-rare, turning 3 or 4 times.

Babe and Kris Winkelman Food Products

When Kris and I began thinking about introducing our own food products, we knew that they had to be the best. Our family and friends have tested the whole line. And just like the passion that we put into our television programs, we made sure that these were premium products available to our fellow anglers and hunters.

We hope our food products help you enjoy your outdoor adventures even more by making your harvest from the woods and water a great experience for your whole family at the table.

These batters, seasonings, jerky mixes and marinades/dipping sauces are designed to enhance wild game—and they're also great with beef, pork, fish and poultry. Look for our food products at a store near you or online at www.winkelman.com.

APPENDIX

A Few Cooking Terms

Bouquet Garni

This classic French herb bundle is used to flavor stocks, sauces or soups while keeping the seasonings from becoming part of the dish.

To prepare: In a small piece of cheesecloth, place 2 small bay leaves, some fresh chopped (or dried) parsley, 1 teaspoon (.75 g) dried thyme, 10 whole black peppercorns and a large clove of crushed garlic. Tie the cheesecloth with a piece of kitchen string. Discard the bouquet garni when the cooking is completed.

Breadcrumbs

Some of the recipes in this cookbook call for fresh breadcrumbs. Making your own not only is less expensive than purchasing prepared crumbs, it also produces a more flavorful product.

To prepare: Cut the crust off fresh bread and process in a blender or a food processor, a few slices at a time.

Clarified Butter

This ingredient is used in several recipes in this cookbook because it burns less easily than regular butter.

To prepare: Melt the butter over very low heat, then pour it into a clear measuring cup and place in the refrigerator. When the butter hardens, scrape off the foam from the top. Place the cup in the microwave and melt the butter again. The butter will separate into two layers: a clear yellow liquid on top, and a milky residue on the bottom. Carefully pour the butter into a cheesecloth-lined strainer, leaving as much of the milky residue as possible in the measuring cup. Save the clear yellow liquid and discard the milky residue.

Cornstarch

This is a popular and useful thickening agent.

To prepare a cornstarch slurry: Add a small amount to cold water or wine, mixing thoroughly. Whichever liquid is used, be certain the cornstarch is thoroughly dissolved in the liquid before adding to the sauce.

Crème Fraîche

Most restaurants use a double cream or crème fraîche rather than the heavy cream available in grocery stores. Crème fraîche has a nutty flavor and can be boiled without curdling.

To prepare: In a saucepan, combine 1 cup (2.3 dl) heavy cream and 1 tablespoon (15 ml) buttermilk. Cook over very low heat (not more than 85°F/29°C), stirring constantly, until warmed. Let the mixture stand at room temperature, loosely covered, until thickened, usually 5 to 8 hours. Store in the refrigerator for up to 10 days.

Deglazing a Pan

As meats are being cooked or browned, they give off flavorful juices that form caramelized bits on the bottom of the pan. Deglazing is a method of incorporating the flavor of these juices into the dish, stock or sauce that accompanies it.

To deglaze: When the meat has been removed from the pan, add a small amount of water, wine, liquor or stock to the hot pan and stir until the accumulated bits have been dissolved into the liquid.

Roasted Garlic

Garlic is the most powerfully flavored member of the onion family, rich in minerals.

To prepare: Cut off the top of an unpeeled head of garlic, rub head with olive oil and place in a baking dish or on a piece of foil. Bake in a 350°F (175°C) oven for 1 hour. Remove from the oven, and set aside until cool enough to handle. Separate the cloves and squeeze the juice and pulp from the skin by pressing with the side of a large knife (or squeeze through a garlic press).

Roux

This is a thickening agent used in sauces and gravies. In most cases, we prefer it to cornstarch or other thickeners. It's easy to make and can be stored in the refrigerator or freezer in plastic food-storage containers. I always have a container in the fridge, ready to use.

To prepare: Melt a measured amount of butter in a saucepan over low heat. Blend in an equal amount of flour, cooking and stirring until the mixture is smooth and develops a nutty aroma, and is colored as you wish.

Most cooks use a white or blonde roux, which takes only minutes to prepare. For dark sauces, a dark roux can be prepared by cooking the roux longer, until it becomes darker. Some chefs prefer to cook roux in a 375°F (190°C) oven for 1 hour, stirring occasionally. The finished product will be very dark in color and have the consistency of sand.

Substitution Charts

In each section of this cookbook, one species of game may be replaced by another similar species.

For example, in the Fish recipe section, northern pike, walleye or muskellunge can be substituted in a recipe that calls for largemouth bass. But for best results, use a fish from the same grouping on the fish substitution chart (below).

The other charts on pages 120-121 also allow substitution for similar types of species within the big game, upland game and waterfowl sections.

Fish Substitution Chart

TYPE	SPECIES NAME	OTHER COMMON NAMES
large oily (2 pounds/900 g or larger)	salmon:	
	chinook	king salmon, tyee
	coho	silver salmon
	sockeye	red salmon
	pink	humpback
	chum	dog salmon
	Atlantic	landlocked salmon, sebago salmon
	trout:	
	brook	squaretail, speckled trout
	brown	Loch Leven trout, German brown
	rainbow	steelhead, Kamloops
	cutthroat	Yellowstone trout
	lake	gray trout, togue, Mackinaw
small oily (up to 2 pounds/900 g)	salmon:	
	Kokanee	sockeye, red salmon
	trout:	
	brook	squaretail, speckled trout
	brown	Loch Leven trout, German brown
	rainbow	steelhead, Kamloops
	cutthroat	Yellowstone trout
large lean (2 pounds/900 g or larger)	black bass:	
	largemouth	black bass
	smallmouth	bronzeback, black bass
	muskellunge	muskie
	northern pike	jack, pickerel, snake
	striped bass	rockfish, striper
	walleye	walleyed pike, pickerel, doré
	white bass	striper, silver bass
small lean (up to 2 pounds/900 g)	panfish:	
	bluegill	bream, sunfish
	yellow perch	ringed perch, striped perch
	crappie	papermouth, speckled perch
	pumpkinseed	bream, sunfish
	black bass:	
	largemouth	black bass
	smallmouth	bronzeback, black bass
	white bass	striper, silver bass
catfish and bullheads	catfish:	
	flathead	yellow cat, mud cat
	channel	fiddler
	blue	white cat, silver cat
	bullhead	horned pout

Big Game Substitution Chart

DEER CUT	TENDERNESS	SUBSTITUTE	COOKING METHOD
tenderloin (whole)	very tender	tenderloin portion from moose, elk or caribou loin portion from caribou, deer or antelope	oven roast, grill
loin (portion)	tender	loin portion from moose, elk or caribou tenderloin (whole) from moose, elk or caribou	oven roast, broil, grill, pan-broil, panfry
loin steak	tender	loin steak from moose, elk or caribou tenderloin from moose, elk, caribou, deer or antelope	broil, grill, pan-broil, panfry
loin chop	tender	loin chop from any big-game animal	broil, grill, pan-broil, panfry
rump roast	intermediate tender	rump roast from any big-game animal deer sirloin tip rolled, tied bottom round from deer or antelope eye of round from moose, elk or caribou	oven roast, grill, braise
round steak	intermediate tender	round steak from any big-game animal sirloin steak from any big-game animal loin chop from moose, elk, caribou, deer or antelope	broil, grill, pan-broil, panfry, stir-fry (strips)
boneless rolled shoulder roast	less tender	boneless rolled shoulder roast from any big-game animal rolled rib roast from moose, elk or caribou boneless chuck roast from moose, elk or caribou	braise
bone-in chuck roast	less tender	bone-in chuck roast from any big-game animal blade pot roast from moose, elk or caribou	braise

Waterfowl Substitution Chart

	SPECIES	APPROXIMATE DRESSED WEIGHT	NUMBER OF SERVINGS	COOKING METHOD
large geese	giant Canada (young)	4 to 6 lbs. (1.8 to 2.7 kg)	4 to 6	oven roast, grill, panfry
	giant Canada (mature)	6½ to 10 lbs. (2.9 to 4.5 kg)	6 to 10	parboil/roast, braise, stew
	interior canada (mature)	4¾ to 6 lbs. (2.2 to 2.7 kg)	5 to 10	parboil/roast, braise, stew
medium-size geese	lesser Canada	3 to 4½ lbs. (1.4 to 2 kg)	3 to 6	oven roast, grill, panfry
	snow or blue goose	3 to 4 lbs. (1.4 to 1.8 kg)	3 to 5	oven roast, grill, panfry
	white-fronted goose	3½ to 3¾ lbs. (1.6 to 1.7 kg)	3 to 5	oven roast, grill, panfry
	interior Canada (young)	3½ to 4½ lbs. (1.6 to 2 kg)	4 to 5	oven roast, grill, panfry
small geese/ large ducks	cackling Canada, brant	1¾ to 2½ lbs. (.8 to 1.1 kg)	2 to 3	oven roast, grill, panfry
	canvasback	1¾ lbs. (793 g)	2	oven roast, grill, panfry
	mallard, black duck	1¼ to 1½ lbs. (570 to 680 g)	2	oven roast, grill, panfry
	redhead, greater scaup	1¼ lbs. (570 g)	2	oven roast, grill, panfry
small ducks	goldeneye, pintail	1 to 1¼ lbs. (450 to 570 g)	1 to 1½	oven roast, grill, panfry
	gadwall, lesser scaup	¾ to 1 lb. (340 to 450 g)	1 to 1½	oven roast, grill, panfry
	widgeon (baldpate)	¾ to 1 lb. (340 to 450 g)	1 to 1½	oven roast, grill, panfry
	ringneck (ringbill)	¾ lb. (340 g)	1 to 1½	oven roast, grill, panfry
	wood duck	½ to ¾ lb. (225 to 340 g)	1	oven roast, grill, panfry
	bufflehead	5 oz. to ¾ lb. (140 to 340 g)	1	oven roast, grill, panfry
	blue-winged teal, cinnamon teal, green-winged teal	5 oz. to ½ lb. (140 to 225 g)	1 or less	oven roast, grill, panfry

Upland Game Substitution Chart

SPECIES	APPROX. DRESSED WEIGHT	NUMBER OF SERVINGS	SUBSTITUTE	COOKING METHOD
wild turkey (whole)	8 to 16 lbs. (3.6 to 7.3 kg)	5 to 10	domestic turkey of similar weight (not prebasted type)	oven roast
wild turkey (any pieces)	3 to 4½ lbs. (1.4 to 2 kg)	6 to 8	2 pheasants, quartered 3 ruffed or sharptail grouse, halved 3 or 4 Chukar or Hungarian partridge, halved 3 lbs. domestic turkey pieces, excess fat removed	panfry, braise, bake
pheasant (whole)	1½ to 2¼ lbs. (.7 to 1 kg)	3 to 4	2 ruffed or sharptail grouse 2 Chukar or Hungarian partridge	oven roast, pan-broil, panfry, braise, bake
2 pheasants (cut up)	3 to 4½ lbs. (1.4 to 2 kg)	6 to 8	thighs and legs from wild turkey 3 or 4 ruffed or sharptail grouse, quartered 4 Chukar or Hungarian partridge, quartered 8 quail, halved	panfry, braise, bake
pheasant (2 whole breasts, boneless)	1 lb. (450 g)	4	boned breast portion or thighs from turkey boned breast and thighs from 2 ruffed or sharptail grouse, 2 Chukar or Hungarian partridge boned breasts from 4 quail boned breasts from 6 or 7 doves	panfry, bake, deep-fry, grill, braise
ruffed or sharptail grouse (whole)	1 to 1¼ lbs. (450 to 570 g)	2 to 3	½ pheasant 1 Chukar or Hungarian partridge	oven roast, panfry, bake, braise, grill
Chukar or Hungarian partridge	¾ to 1 lb. (340 to 450 g)	2	½ pheasant 1 ruffed or sharptail grouse	oven roast, panfry, bake, braise
quail	4 quail (4 to 6 oz./110 to 170 g each)	4	1 pheasant, cut up 1½ ruffed or sharptail grouse, cut up 2 Chukar or Hungarian partridge, quartered	oven roast, panfry, bake, braise, grill
woodcock	5 to 6 woodcock, (5 oz./ 140 g each)	4	1 pheasant, cut up 1½ ruffed grouse, cut up 2 Chukar or Hungarian partridge, cut up 4 quail, halved	panfry, braise, bake
dove	6 or 7 doves (2 to 3 oz./ 55 to 85 g each)	4	1 pheasant, cut up, breast section halved 1½ ruffed or sharptail grouse, cut up, breast sections halved 2 Chukar or Hungarian partridge, cut up, breast sections halved 4 quail, halved	panfry, braise, bake

NUTRITION INFORMATION

	Calories	Fat (g)	Sodium (mg)	Saturated Fat (g)	Protein (g)	Carbohydrate (g)	Cholesterol (mg)
Apple Cinnamon Duck	281	9	113	3	39	9	153
Bacon-Wrapped Backstrap w/Sauce	239	6	481	2	37	9	93
Baked Crappie Divine	300	24	300	15	21	0	158
Baked Fish w/Honey-Lemon Sauce	247	13	174	6	25	7	111
Baked Pheasant w/Asparagus	364	13	727	4	29	33	57
Baked Walleye	340	22	293	13	33	1	201
Barbecue Meatballs	346	15	1,069	7	21	29	132
Barbecue Sauce	31	1	163	1	0	5	3
Barbecue Venison	537	6	1,976	2	55	70	191
Bass Dill Dip	31	2	56	0	3	1	7
BBQ Northern Fillets	183	2	323	0	34	6	66
Big Game Chislic	136	6	269	1	18	1	64
Bob Mitchell's Venison Marinade	336	31	785	4	1	15	0
Braised Canada Goose w/Sauce	570	40	419	14	42	7	159
Braised Gamebird Supreme	549	36	1,243	21	26	30	140
Broiled Hunan Bass Fillets	159	6	851	1	22	2	77
Butt Kickin' Barbecue	397	8	674	2	36	44	129
Cabbage-and-Garlic Mashed Potatoes	164	4	572	2	4	30	10
Cajun Catfish	341	13	1,011	3	33	21	189
Cajun Catfish Tortellini	812	45	1,403	24	53	47	238
Cajun Walleye	389	15	146	5	36	25	162
Catfish Italian Style	671	31	440	17	34	59	133
Coconut Crappie	376	19	162	6	35	14	149
Crappie w/Shrimp Dip	218	10	170	3	30	1	152
Cream of Morel Soup	188	17	756	10	3	5	48
Creamed Wild Turkey	398	26	929	16	29	10	125
Creamy Braised Upland Bird	1,048	88	469	50	29	38	321
Creamy Mushroom Soup	374	32	638	17	8	17	82
Crispy Stuffed Fish	298	17	352	9	26	8	123
Crunchy Mashed Sweet Potatoes	497	11	495	6	8	89	129
Deep-Fried Wild Turkey	846	40	291	11	114	0	331
Delta Baked Fish	407	11	684	6	35	38	170
Duck Delights	451	33	1,095	15	14	24	85
Easy Baked Fish w/Mushroom Sauce	351	18	744	9	32	14	137
Easy Oven Crappies	165	3	109	1	27	6	156
Easy Waterfowl Appetizer	216	10	3,545	4	19	13	49
Elaine's Duck	438	26	2,435	7	25	25	88
Fall-Off-the-Bone Venison Pot Roast	364	9	184	2	48	20	169
Fast Crappie Gumbo	413	14	547	8	34	39	162
Finger-Licking Venison Ribs	908	9	2,329	3	79	131	287
Fish and Crab Cakes	211	14	248	5	13	8	64
Fish Cakes	483	20	992	9	20	55	87
Fish Croquettes	276	19	468	3	10	17	60
Fish Delight	581	45	532	17	36	8	171
Fish in Wine Sauce	429	31	553	17	32	5	179
Fish Pizza	342	12	451	4	17	36	71
Foiled Venison Chops	356	8	91	2	34	37	108
Fresh Fish Hash	376	22	309	7	31	11	118
Gamebird Alfredo	1,271	88	1,405	50	52	73	315
Gamebird Marsala	625	44	278	23	22	21	148
Gamebird Tetrazzini	475	21	1,660	10	31	38	88
Gamebird–Wild Rice Soup	352	13	1,014	7	21	36	63
Garlic-Herb Mashed Potatoes	133	7	111	5	3	16	18
Gourmet Duck	496	27	336	16	21	44	138
Governor's Venison Recipe	226	10	404	4	31	2	117
Grilled Walleye	147	5	151	3	23	0	114
Halibut Stuffed w/Crab Meat	514	26	491	15	53	14	142
Hidden Valley Fish	582	42	896	10	28	21	129

NUTRITION
122

	Calories	Fat (g)	Sodium (mg)	Saturated Fat (g)	Protein (g)	Carbohydrate (g)	Cholesterol (mg)
Hot Northern Salad	717	51	742	15	45	20	314
Incredibly Easy Venison Pot Roast	247	9	228	4	36	4	137
It's in the Bag	554	30	524	10	40	30	147
Jeff's Fabulous Pheasant	872	68	667	41	28	36	263
Jim Zumbo's Ginger Elk	222	5	842	1	28	15	62
Kris' Marinade	3	0	583	0	0	1	0
Lemon-Butter Sauce	139	15	7	9	0	1	45
Lemon-Dill Sauce	75	8	2	5	0	1	22
Marinated Duck Breast w/Bacon	109	5	205	1	11	4	41
Mashed Potatoes and Sweet Potatoes	285	9	106	5	4	48	22
Mexican Walleye	440	23	1,674	8	37	20	154
Mexican Wild Turkey	1,209	74	2,278	38	54	79	232
Minnesota Marinade	43	4	127	0	0	1	0
Morels and Stuffing	289	18	540	10	6	26	78
Mushroom-Baked Fish	401	29	355	16	33	1	178
Mushroom-Cream Sauce	57	5	48	3	0	1	13
Mushroom-Port Sauce	67	6	30	4	1	2	22
Mustard-Butter Sauce	77	8	10	5	0	1	23
Northern Pike w/Dill Sauce	500	23	907	13	46	25	190
Ocean Fish Marinade	16	0	552	0	1	3	0
Oriental Grouse Salad	570	46	968	7	24	20	58
Outpost Lodge Pheasant	231	7	55	2	22	19	47
Oven-Crispy Walleye	303	14	369	8	38	4	212
Parmesan Fish w/Alfredo Sauce	1,032	70	1,091	39	52	50	356
Parmesan Walleye w/Champagne	811	44	506	25	59	36	475
Pecan Catfish	735	53	292	14	38	29	218
Peking Gamebird	180	3	1,056	1	20	20	45
Pheasant Bundles	470	39	223	22	9	21	123
Pheasant Cordon Bleu Casserole	483	31	1,217	16	30	20	118
Pheasant Dinner Pie	782	47	887	23	20	64	122
Pheasant Forever	724	59	75	33	25	24	224
Pheasant Phingers	684	40	694	23	38	42	238
Pineapple-Basil Sauce	43	4	4	3	0	1	15
Plain Wild Rice	154	1	378	0	7	30	0

	Calories	Fat (g)	Sodium (mg)	Saturated Fat (g)	Protein (g)	Carbohydrate (g)	Cholesterol (mg)
Plum Dandy Port Sauce	24	1	58	1	0	2	4
Pressured Goose	1,372	124	1,073	36	58	1	295
Quail w/Rice	907	62	1,801	29	47	40	267
Roast Goose Breast	315	15	408	5	35	5	130
Sautéed Venison Steak in Sauce	352	20	402	11	40	2	193
Seasoned Fried Quail	493	31	556	7	30	21	106
Spinach-Stuffed Fish Rolls	285	14	318	6	36	3	135
"Squashed" Potatoes	285	19	197	11	3	29	50
Stuffed Elk Peppers	407	21	672	10	34	20	105
Stuffed, Bacon-Wrapped Gamebird w/Sauce	621	31	1,119	13	49	27	138
"Stuffed" Stuffing	802	36	1,163	20	37	86	176
Sue's Fish and Chips	301	18	261	9	30	3	152
Sweet, Simple Orange Sauce #1	138	5	308	3	1	24	12
Sweet, Simple Orange Sauce #2	23	0	84	0	0	3	0
Sweet, Simple Orange Sauce #3	46	3	154	2	0	3	8
Sweet, Simple Orange Sauce #4	54	0	180	0	0	13	0
Taco Fish	339	17	268	5	31	15	160
Tarragon Venison Backstrap	453	29	299	16	43	3	185
Thai Fish	366	21	520	4	39	2	147
Toasted Fish Appetizer	448	28	650	17	22	27	118
Venison Enchiladas	515	20	1,995	7	33	49	102
Venison Meatballs	441	30	591	15	34	7	221
Venison Stew	305	5	1,797	1	25	39	66
Venison Stroganoff	447	24	661	14	41	15	183
Venison–Wild Rice Soup	198	7	669	3	16	18	53
Walleye-Wild Rice Cakes	432	35	294	18	16	13	226
Warm Fish Appetizer	379	29	268	17	24	5	129
Wild Rice & Mushroom Risotto	547	20	1,792	8	18	70	25
Wild Rice and Mushrooms	107	5	9	3	3	14	12
Wild Rice Soufflé	816	58	606	35	16	60	197
Wild Rice Soup	675	45	1,611	24	27	40	135
Wild Turkey and Stuffing	1,287	65	1,348	26	130	34	481
Yogurt Crappies	334	16	1,343	6	27	18	195
Yogurt Gamebird w/Cream Sauce	592	46	902	30	24	18	181

INDEX

Creative Publishing international
is your complete source for fish and wild game cookbooks.

Available cooking titles:

- America's Favorite Fish Recipes
- America's Favorite Wild Game Recipes
- Babe & Kris Winkleman's Great Fish & Game Recipes
- Cooking Wild in Kate's Camp
- Cooking Wild in Kate's Kitchen
- Dressing & Cooking Wild Game
- Game Bird Cookery
- The New Cleaning & Cooking Fish
- Preparing Fish & Wild Game
- The Saltwater Cookbook
- Venison Cookery

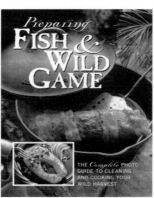
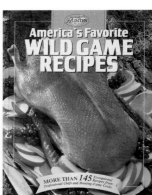

To purchase these or other titles, contact your local bookseller, or visit our web site at **www.creativepub.com**.